Stories
of
African American
Struggles
&
Achievements
that Feed the Soul

Dedication

This book is dedicated to all keepers of our Culture who tell our stories by any means necessary.

Ase'

Thank You

Special thanks to all members of Nathaniel Gadsden's Writers Wordshop, past and present, who inspire me each and every day.

Thanks to Author & Publisher Terri D. for making this book a reality and a blessing!

Special thanks to Rev. Christopher Thomas, founder, and Director of The Voice 17104 Harrisburg & The Voice TV, for hosting the Writers Wordshop's weekly reading platform.

Special Thanks to The Pennsylvania Council On the Arts, for providing funding and technical assistance to the Writers Wordshop over the years.

Special thanks to Patricia Gadsden, my beautiful & intelligent wife, for being my help mate and cheerleader in everything I do!

Special thanks to Black Wall Street Newspaper of Harrisburg, PA.

About the author

Rev. Dr. Nathaniel Gadsden

Rev. Dr. Nathaniel Gadsden, Pastor of Life Esteem Ministries, Redeemed Christian Church of God, is a certified Family Development Training and Credentialing Program Portfolio Advisor. He is also a certified Spiritual Advisor, Chaplain, and Death Doula. He lives in Harrisburg, Pa. with his wife Patricia Gadsden, who is founder of Life Esteem Inc., and the Life Esteem Holistic Health and Wellness Center.

He is retired from the Pennsylvania Department of Education, as State Director of the Higher Education Equal Opportunity Program (ACT 101), and as Community Impact Manager, and Director of the Fatherhood Academy for the United Way of the Capital Region. Rev. Gadsden currently works as a part-time Chaplain for UPMC West Shore Hospital. He is a Christian Therapist and author of "Learning Self Therapy through Writing" a creative writing journal, "By Any Words Necessary" a collection of his poetry, "Candy From Heaven" his first children's book, and "All Things Considered" a collection of his poetry and essays. He is Co-Host, with his wife Patricia, of the Life Esteem Television Show, which airs on WHP-TV 21 (CBS). He is also host of three weekly Facebook Life Shows on "The Voice 17104.Harrisburg." Rev. Gadsden is a contributing writer for the Black Wall Street News Paper.

Rev. Dr. Nathaniel Gadsden and his wife Patricia are proud parents of six adult children, twenty-two grandchildren and six great grandchildren.

Table of Contents

Introduction...7

Spiritual Foundation – The Inner Journey...9

Coach Larry Moore: A Winner by Any Standard...12

Black Kid Magic: It's a Family Venture 14

NAACP ACT-SO: Olympics of the Mind 16

Pastor Joe Summers: Spreading God's Word World-Wide 19

Black History 365: August 21

Doakes and Soaps: The Clean-Up Lady 25

Harrisburg PAL: Still Going Strong 26

Let the Word Be Heard..29

Kwanzaa: An African American Holiday 32

Keep Youth Out of Adult Prisons..34

Meet Dr. Ericka S. Pinckney...36

Miriam Makeba 37

NuBorn Skin: Love the Skin You're In 40

Nyeusi Print Shop: Black Owned/Black Excellence...42

Our Trip to South Africa: Thank You Dr. Yates...44

Protest and Repercussions 46

Rafiyqa Muhammad: An Agent for Change 48

Reginald F. Lewis, Esq." Keep Going, No Matter What."....................................50

She Grabbed Me 53

Shirley Chisholm: A Renowned Renegade...55

Stop the Violence: Is it Still a Movement 58

The African Burial Ground 61

What, So What, Now What...64

An Engaged Father Matters 67

Porter's House Jamaican Restaurant **69**

Claudette Colvin: Before Rosa Parks Sat.. **72**

Come by Here Lord **73**

A Memorial on My Bucket List **76**

Anthony & Melisa: They Keep Believing... **79**

How I Enter Matters.. **81**

Pandemic Diary **82**

You Don't See What I See... **84**

Introduction

By Rev. Dr. Nathaniel Gadsden

This book is a labor of love. Most of the articles were written for my monthly commitment to the Black Wall Street Newspaper, which is published in Harrisburg, Pennsylvania. This free publication is dedicated to highlighting people, places, and events in the African American community in Central Pennsylvania. Many of my articles also highlighted historical leaders, national and international institutions, and important events in African American history.

This book is a compilation of articles written over a two-year period, coupled with some of my spoken word pieces, and African Proverbs that make me think. I am mostly motivated to write by my love of African American history, and the study of the African diaspora. Another reason I was motivated to publish this book, is because of the many people, who I have written about, that will be introduced to a wider audience. My hope is that this book will inspire you, the reader, to understand that African American history is happening around us every day. Also, African American leaders are with us in many forms, and it is up to us to recognize them, and support them, as best we can.

Another factor that I hope you, the reader of this book, will realize is that you are a leader and a history maker in your own right. With the recent mantra "Black Lives Matter," we, have the opportunity, to ask ourselves how does Black Lives Matter? Do we really believe that Black Lives Matter, especially considering, the rate of black-on-black crimes, poorly rated public schools in our communities, mistrust of black institutions and "leaders" in our communities, and do black people still prefer to live in a black community?

As I stated at the beginning of this introduction, this book is a labor of love for me, because I have truly enjoyed putting together these articles, personal photographs, African Proverbs and spoken word pieces. I don't always find it easy to write my articles and my spoken word/poetry. It takes effort on my part to start the writing process. Once I get started, I find it hard to stop. I always enter in a zone that, I personally believe, is inspired by our ancestors. I define myself as an African American writer. I have always defined myself as an African American writer. I am inspired by everything African, African American, Black, and BIPOC (Black, Indigenous, people of color). I love interacting and studying various cultures and ethnic groups. I have taught Cultural Competence, and Cultural Humility on the college level. I am a proud member of the World Affairs Council of Central Pennsylvania. I served as co-chair of the Mayor's Interfaith Council of Harrisburg, PA, for eight years.

In 1977, I founded Nathaniel Gadsden's Writers Wordshop, which is dedicated to providing a platform for writers of all Genre. Also, the Wordshop is open to all persons, regardless of race, age, sexual orientation, and educational background. The Writers Wordshop encourages all, who take advantage of our weekly open readings, to find their voice and use it. We use the famous poem, by Poet Jayne Cortez, "Find Your Own Voice" as our motto. I found my voice in my pain, struggles, low self-esteem, achievements, and victories of my life. I found my voice in the storytelling of Ebony and Jet magazines. I found my voice in the great writings of African American Poets, especially those revolutionary voices of the 1960's, 70's and 80's, such as Sonia Sanchez, Amiri Baraka, Haki Madhubuti, Gil Scott-Hearn, Maya Angelou, and The Last Poets. I was, and I still am, lifted-up by great African and African American writers who tell our story by telling their story. I read and study writers and poets, from my community, who have a perspective on issues and concerns in my community. These writers have helped me find my voice and use it. I hope and pray this book, and the stories in it, will inspire you to find and use your voice in a positive way to make our world a better place.

Spiritual Foundation – The Inner Journey

By Rev. Dr. Nathaniel Gadsden

I am a firm believer that a good foundation in life begins with one's spiritual perspective or spiritual lens. In my book "Learning Self-Therapy Through Writing: an experience in creative journaling", I discuss the four bridges that we must all learn to cross in order to be confident, connected and in control of the path we determine to travel in life. The first bridge that I believe we must cross is the bridge of "I Am." The Bridge of I Am is where you come to grips with who you are, and how you feel about yourself, it is the fundamental arena in which beliefs about "self" are created and nurtured. To identify what "I Am" means is step one toward becoming the person you desire to be. It is the area in which you discover why you think of yourself as you do, and what things over your lifetime have brought you to your conclusions.

The importance of the self-concept in an individual goes far beyond providing a basis for one's reality. The self-image begins to form very early in life. In infancy, we constantly explore ourselves and the world around us. We learn what is "me" and what is "not me" and discover we are a separate being. We learn to respond to our own name and acquire a sense of our own identity.

The next bridge is the bridge of "I Can." This bridge may seem to loom larger than the one you've crossed already. Here is where, with a more sure-footed stance, you begin to garner the determination that you can make choices about your life.

For many of us, The Bridge of I Can is a tricky one to cross over! While the previous Bridge of I Am helped us to pinpoint who we believe we are and what is important to us, it now becomes necessary to believe we have the ability to affect that which is important to us. The question becomes, "I know who I am, and I know what I want, but do I really believe I can make it happen?"

The next bridge is the bridge of "I Want To." This bridge is always on our minds yet taking action and actually crossing over is quite another story! The key to crossing the bridge of I Want To is learning to internalize and clarify exactly what it is you want to do, or change or feel, or say, or think, or learn – and developing the wherewithal to accomplish it! Here it is necessary to determine your goals. This is the only way to be clear about what it is you want to do once you cross the bridge. In approaching the bridge of I Want To, be sure to bring along your goals outline – which means spending a little time defining what your goals are. Your goals must be realistic, specific, measurable, have objectives with timelines, and be both short and long-term.   A trap many of us encounter in goal attainment is that once we've reached a goal, we fail to reset new goals. When this happens, feelings of "slippage" or lack of progress can feel overwhelming. Remember, as you set goals for your life, it is wise to do so in stages, so that you are not likely to feel stuck and unproductive.

The next bridge is the bridge of "I'll Do It Today," which deals with a problem that haunts practically everyone at some point in their lives. It is procrastination! Sometimes procrastination can mean putting off until tomorrow what you can do today, or it can mean putting off until next week – month – next year – millennium that which can be done today!
Webster's New World Thesaurus lists these words along with procrastination: drag, linger, trail, poke, dally, tarry, dawdle, loiter. It also says to proceed in a dilatory fashion.

Sometimes we miss opportunities because our past learning styles keep us from seeing certain things that are right in our paths. We develop blind spots too new opportunities because they don't fit our perceptions of the way things are. And all too often, we put off and put off that which we could do today. When this happens, our spiritual foundation begins to weaken, and doubt begins to overwhelm us. It becomes imperative for us to learn to eliminate some of the excuses, reasons, rationales, justifications, and explanations we often use, which impede our growth and success.

There is a poem that I use in the back of my book "Learning Self Therapy Through Writing" entitled "Build A Better World." (Author Unknown) which goes like this:

"Build a better world," said God.
And I answered,
"How? The world is such a vast place,
And so complicated now,
And I am small and helpless,
There's nothing I can do."
But, God in all His wisdom, said,
"Just build a better you."

To all my brothers and sisters, that's all you need to do, just build a better you.
  Let the journey begin. Ase'

If the elders leave you a legacy of dignified language, you do not abandon it and speak childish language.
Ghanaian Proverb

Coach Larry Moore: A Winner by Any Standard

By Rev. Dr. Nathaniel Gadsden

He is best known as Coach, because he coached the Girls basketball team for 14 years at Harrisburg High School, winning 244 games, 32 straight during the 2003-2004 season. He also coached the Girls basketball team for two years at Central Dauphin East High School. Larry Moore is a legendary Coach in Girls basketball throughout Pennsylvania, and a winner by any standard. When you first meet him, you quickly realize that he is a confident, straight-forward man with a great sense of humor. He has the rare quality that some people possess called the "It Factor." You can't explain what "It" is, but you know it is there. I can only imagine that his confident, straight-forward manner, coupled with a great sense of humor and that "It Factor," made him the outstanding coach he became.

Coach Moore began his coaching career as an Assistant Boys Coach at Williamsport High School, Williamsport, Pennsylvania, where he coached for 14 years. It was Harrisburg's good fortune that Coach Moore was encouraged to move to the Capitol City some thirty years ago by his parents. His impact has been tremendous both on and off the court. Coach Moore is also best known as Director of Dauphin County's Department of Parks and Recreation, where he helped to develop and implement the Annual Dauphin County Cultural Festival and the Annual Dauphin County Wine & Jazz Festivals, which garnered national attention for Dauphin County.

On Wednesday, July 6, 2022, Coach Moore officially retired as Head Basketball Coach of the Girls Basketball team of Harrisburg High School. His announcement was made before family members, current and former players, colleagues, friends, and admires. The accolades were many and well deserving. Coach Moore guided his 32-0, undefeated Lady Cougars to the State Finals, where they fell short on the score board, but gained respect as one of the greatest teams, Boys or Girls, to every represent the city of Harrisburg. Also, while coaching Central Dauphin East High School Girls basketball team, his Lady Panthers were ranked 14th in the nation by USA Today. Coach Moore is quick to point out that 90% of the girls he coached in the Harrisburg area went to college. Anyone that knows Coach Moore, knows that he values family, education, hard work, and a good laugh. The outpouring of love and appreciation given to him during his retirement ceremony was heartfelt and sincere.

When I think of Coach Moore, I think of a person who is a "Man's Man." I see other men, including myself, appreciate and respect him as a leader and mentor. He is someone that is not stuck back in time. He has a beautiful, intelligent, wife, and an equally beautiful and intelligent daughter, both of whom are always by his side and supportive of his many activities in the community. It is easy to see that he respects and loves his family, and they respect and love him. Professional, intact, Black family love isn't always portrayed in our community, but it does exist, and the Moore family proves it. I also appreciate that Coach Moore is a creator of events and programs in our community that are wholesome, uplifting, and open to everyone that enjoys good soul music, good food and great fellowship. Over the past few years my wife Pat and I have attended most of the soiree gatherings promoted by Coach Moore and his family. We have always enjoyed ourselves.

I hope and pray that Coach Moore and his family will continue to reside in the Harrisburg area. I know that whatever he decides to use his time and talent for in the days ahead will have great impact on our community. Coach Moore is and has always been more than just a Coach, he is a winner and a leader by any standard of measurement. And to that I say, thanks Coach Moore. You gave us just what we needed.

He who learns teaches.
Ethiopian Proverb

Black Kid Magic: It's a Family Venture
By Rev. Dr. Nathaniel Gadsden

Writing a book is no small feat. Writing two books as a family project is even more difficult, but oh, so rewarding. Ask Tirzah McClinton, co-author of Black Kid Magic, Young, Black, and Making History (Girls Edition), and Black Kid Magic, Young, Black, and Making History (Boys Edition), Esquire Publications.

When ask whose idea was it to write the books, Mrs. McClinton said, "The idea started when my twins were younger and I saw that there weren't many inspirational children's books to choose from, with black and brown characters in them. We started writing during COVID, as a family project, and since my daughter Serayah is a talented artist, and my youngest, Andrew, is interested in becoming a writer, I thought it might be a good experience for them. Serayah, illustrated both books and Andrew co-wrote the Boys Edition with me. Honestly, the books wouldn't be what they are without the addition of their amazing gifts."

I ask Mrs. McClinton, what is the main theme of the books, and she said," That every young person has strengths, passions, and abilities they can use to be changemakers in their communities, and in the world. I hope that black and brown children will see themselves through the young people highlighted in our books and be inspired to act now to use their gifts." She also made it very clear that this is her first book project, but certainly not her last. When I ask her if she plans to do a sequel to "Black Kid Magic", she said, "The Boys Edition was the sequel to the Girls Edition. However, I do plan to write more books with similar themes, highlighting character with black and brown faces. There can never be enough of this literature for our children to read. My ultimate goal is to partner with public libraries and schools locally, and across the country, to place books on as many shelves as we can."

There has been a lot of discussion in recent years about the value of diversity in all segments of society. Research overwhelmingly concludes that children of color relate to, and benefit from, literature that reflects characters that look like them.

The self-esteem of a child is elevated when they can see themselves being the main character, or at least taking part, in the story. I can personally relate to this, being a child of the 1950's, when the only character, of color, I can remember in any of our elementary books was "Little Black Sambo." I can't speak for all, of the children that I attended school with, but I don't think any of my classmates could relate to "Little Black Sambo." In fact, we were ashamed of that character, because we had to contrast him against the fictional life of "Dick, Jane, and Sally" who lived with their mother and father, in a beautiful suburban home with a white picket fence, and of course a family dog. Remembering the point that Mrs. McClinton stated, which is, we need literature featuring people with black and brown faces, so that black and brown children can be inspired to use their gifts.

Mrs. McClinton, who was born in Nassau, Bahamas, and came to the United States when she was 13 years old, received her bachelor's degree from Wake Forest University, and was employed with the Commonwealth of Pennsylvania for 20 years. She now works as a Public Health Analyst at the Federal level, for the US Department of Health and Human Services. I ask her, who influenced you as a writer, she said, "I can't say that I have been influenced by one particular author, I would just say instead, that different individuals, my parents, and mentors I have had overtime, helped me recognize my ability as a writer. Writing has opened many doors for me to use my gifts, and I love it! Writing for children though has by far, been the most gratifying experience of them all.

Finally, I ask her who should read their books, and she said "The format is meant to target younger, elementary-aged readers, but we have received feedback from adults who were also inspired and found the content in our books to be very informative. We hope that parents will take time to read the book with children and help them to begin thinking about their own unique gifts and abilities, and how they can use them to serve a greater purpose.

We do not inherit the earth from our ancestors; we borrow it from our children.
Haida Proverb

NAACP ACT-SO: Olympics of the Mind
By: Rev. Dr. Nathaniel Gadsden

To some it is the best kept secret in America. To others it is an opportunity that has already had a major impact on their lives. The NAACP ACT-SO Competition, founded in 1978 by author and journalist Vernon Jarrett, is intended to provide recognition to young students of African descent, and students of color, who demonstrate academic, scientific, and artistic achievement in one of 33 different categories of competition.

The ACT-SO program is an enrichment program. Over the course of each year students work with local volunteer instructors and mentors to develop projects, and sharpen their skills to participate in enrichment opportunities, including workshops, tutorials, and field trips specific to their competitions. The local competitions and ceremonies showcase the results of the student's hard work. Competition winners receive medals and prizes provided by local and regional sponsors and contributors. The local Gold Medalists are eligible to advance to the national competition and have the opportunity to win a medal, receive scholarships and other rewards provided by the national sponsors.

The Greater Harrisburg NAACP ACT-SO program, directed by Mr. Kaaba Brunson, has a long rich history in this competition that dates-back to the 1990's, and continues today. In recent years, the Greater Harrisburg NAACP ACT-SO program has produced three national medal winners and one $10,00 national scholarship award winner. In 2020, Poet Lunden McClain, currently a Freshmen at Indiana University of Pennsylvania, won a bronze medal in the Poetry Written category. In 2022, Madison Stokes, currently a Freshmen a Chatham University, won a gold medal in the medicine category. Also, in 2022, Tijesuni Ademuwagun currently a senior at Milton Hershey School, won a bronze medal in the traditional-dance category. Another student, Danneil Mubbala, currently a Freshmen at the University of Pittsburgh, won a $10,000 scholarship for an essay she wrote for the ACT-SO competition.

The scholarship was sponsored by the Oscar winning actress Lupita Nyong'o, who is best known for her roles in the movies 12 Years A Slave, and Black Panther. Danneil Mubbala was one of 40 young women, selected from around the country, to receive the scholarship.

The local and national ACT-SO competitions for 2023 are fast approaching. Students in grades 9th through 12th are encouraged to apply. All area school districts will be notified of the local competition's student application process, mentoring opportunities, date and times of the competition, and categories that the students can compete in. Interested students should check with the main office in their school to inquire if the school has applications, or if there is an ACT-SO coordinator in their building. All interested persons can go to the Greater Harrisburg NAACP ACT-SO webpage (Harrisburg, PA ACT-SO), and register for the 2023 local competition.

Participating students can select up to 3 categories to compete in. There are 6 major areas of competition, STEM (Science, Technology, Engineering, & Math): Humanities: The Performing Arts: The Visual Arts: Business: & Culinary. The categories are listed under each major competition area on the webpage. Once students have registered and selected their areas of interest they will be notified by the ACT-SO committee to make sure they, and their parents, have completed all required paperwork, and answer any questions they may have.

Since its inception, almost 400,000 young people have participated in the ACT-SO program, and more than 900 gold medals have been awarded to youths from around the United States. Some of the notable ACT-SO alumni are actor Anthony Anderson, singers Lauryn Hill and Alicia Keys, Astronaut Mae Jamison, movie director John Singleton, singer Michelle Williams, rapper Kanye West, actress Jada Pinkett-Smith, and singer/actress Jennifer Hudson.

As chairperson of the local judges committee, I am asking our adult community to support the NAACP program goals for ACT-SO, which are the promotion of classroom and after-school excellence; recognize academic achievement among our youth on par with the recognition awarded to athletics; to provide and assist students with the necessary skills and tools to establish goals and acquire the confidence and training to make a successful contribution to society.

Having read this article, you are now a Mandated Supporter of the Greater Harrisburg NAACP ACT-SO Program. You are mandated to encourage as many students as you can to participate in this excellent competition. Thank you for your service.

No matter how full the river, it still wants to grow.
Congolese Proverb

Pastor Joe Summers: Spreading God's Word World-Wide
By: Rev. Dr. Nathaniel Gadsden

Pastor Joseph Summers, former Director of the Black Achievers Program of the Camp Curtin YMCA in Harrisburg, Pennsylvania, has been living and teaching in China for almost 15 years. Rev. Summers first moved to China to teach English to Chinese students. After establishing himself in his profession, and fully immersing into the Chinese culture, he created his own school of education, and began to pastor a church that included many university-level African students studying in China. Pastor Summers also found time to visit many parts of Africa, and even helped to build a school for children in Kenya, East Africa.

Pastor Summers has a passion for teaching the Gospel of Jesus Christ. Before leaving Harrisburg, he had established a church congregation that had at its core a teaching ministry. As he transitioned to China, he took that same vision and mission with him. Today, Pastor Summers is the founder and President of Jinan International Christian Fellowship Bible Institute (JICFBI), which is an out-growth of his ministry, Jinan International Christian Fellowship (JICF). If you go to the JICFBI webpage, you will discover that the ministry and Bible Institute is comprised predominantly of students from various countries around the world who travel to China for further studies. A significant number of these students come from countries in Africa. The major focus of JICF is to provide spiritual support for the students, support mission work, with the focal point being the development of leaders so that students have the skills, and resources, necessary to assist in other fellowships around China as well as providing leadership when they return home.

Pastor Summers through his JICF ministry established the JICF Bible Institute in conjunction with Harvestime International Network. Harvestime provided the curriculum resources that JICF Bible Institute needed. Harvestime stresses that the challenge for laborers for the spiritual harvest fields of the world is greater than ever as we near the return of our Lord and Savior, Jesus Christ. The only way this great spiritual harvest will be reaped is for each born-again believer to become a reproducing Christian-a harvester. It is to this vision Harvestime International Network and the JICF Bible Institute is dedicated to raising up laborers for worldwide spiritual harvest.

The JICF Bible Institute statement of faith is "The Bible Institute is a non-denominational training center that encourages the participation of all who profess Christian belief. While there are several aspects of the Bible that may be open for discussion and interpretation, the institute relies on certain indisputable facts: Christ Came, Christ Died, Christ Rose, and Christ is coming back again."

The Bible Institute does not replace the church. Believers will continue to meet in their home churches. The JICF Bible Institute is an extension of the church. Students should know that the Institute does not replace the ministry of the church but extends it. The purpose of the institute is not to replace any existing institution actively spreading the Gospel.

Some of the teaching faculty at JICFBI are Mike Wood, who has been in ministry for over 35 years, and has helped train pastors in Haiti. Pastor Irungu Kiiru of Kenya, who is overseeing 15 Churches of the Redeemed Gospel Church ministry. Dr. Life Mashumba, who served under the Botswana Ministry for Education over 21 years. Pastor Davin Naidoo of Yahweh International Christian Worship Center, Pietermaritzburg, South Africa. Pastor Joseph Summers Founder of JICF Ministry and JICF Bible Institute. And me, Pastor Nathaniel Gadsden, Life Esteem Ministries Redeemed Christian Church of God, Harrisburg, PA.

The JICF Bible Institute offers a Certificate Program, requires six courses, which takes about a year. The Diploma Program requires 12 courses, which takes about 2 years. The Degree Program requires 18 courses, and a 45-minute sermon/lesson, which takes about 3 years. All of the courses are offered through zoom.

Knowledge without wisdom is like water in the sand.
Guinean Proverb

Black History 365: August

By Rev. Dr. Nathaniel Gadsden

One month cannot tell our story. Perhaps 100 years cannot tell our story. The story of African people the world over is a story that, in many ways, has yet to be fully told. The celebration of Black History month each year is a needed and necessary reminder that we contributed to world history, and not just American history. The problem is, and has always been from the beginning, that we have greatly limited the scope of our celebration to just a few names, and a few events, which we recite over-and-over again. Case in point, the destruction of "Black Wall Street" in Tulsa, Oklahoma in 1921, was "uncovered" and greatly explored in 2021, 100 years later. Many people of African descent admitted that they had never heard of the "Black Wall Street Massacre."

My wife, Patricia "Pat" Gadsden, founder of Life Esteem Inc., and the Life Esteem Holistic Health & Wellness Center, every year collects calendars that list important dates in Black History. The calendars have important information that we should further research in order to fully understand the significance our history has to world history. The calendars also have wonderful artwork that I find worthy of collecting each year.

Did you know that Ronald H. Brown, the first African American to head the Democratic National Committee, was born August 1, 1941.? There was a Charter school in Harrisburg, PA. named after this great political leader. Sadly, Secretary Brown was killed in a plane crash in 1996, near Dubrovnik, Croatia.

August 2, 2012, Gabrielle Douglas becomes the first African American to win the women's All-Around and team Olympic gold medals in gymnastics.

August 4, 1961, Barack Obama, the 1ˢᵗ African American President of the United States of America, is born. In the estimation of many, Barack Obama is considered one of the greatest Presidents in the history of the United States.

August 5, 1914, the first electric traffic lights invented by Garrett Morgan (a black inventor), were installed at Euclid Ave. and 105th Street, Cleveland, Ohio.

August 6, 1965, President Lyndon Johnson signs the Voting Rights Bill, which made it possible for millions of African American citizens to vote in local, state, and national elections.

August 7, 1903, Ralph Bunche, the first African American Noble Prize winner, is born.

August 8, 1866, Matthew Henson, explorer and first to reach the North Pole, is born.

August 9, 1936, Jesse Owens wins four Olympic gold medals in Berlin, Germany.

August 9, 1869, Anne Turnbo Malone, inventor of the first pressing comb in 1900, is born.

August 10, 1989, Gen. Colin Powell is nominated as Chairman of the Joint Chiefs of Staff.

August 11, 1921, Alex Haley, author of Roots, is born. Roots became a bestselling book and a television mini-series that totally captivated a world-wide audience for an entire week.

August 11, 1965, the Watts riots begin.

August 11, 2016, Simone Manuel becomes the first Black woman to win an individual gold in Olympic swimming.

August 12, 1922, Frederick Douglas's home in Washington, D.C. is declared a national memorial.

August 14, 1959, Ervin" Magic" Johnson, basketball hall of famer and entrepreneur, is born.

August 14, 1966, Halle Berry, first African American woman to win an Oscar for best actress, is born.

August 15, 1824, Liberia, Africa, is established by freed enslaved African Americans.
August 15, 1938, Maxine Waters, U.S. Congresswoman, is born.

August 15, 2016, Allyson Felix becomes the most decorated female track & field athlete in American history.

August 16, 1947, Carol Moseley-Braun, the first African American woman in the U.S. Senate, is born.

August 17, 1887, Marcus Garvey, Black Nationalist, is born.

August 19, 1989, Bishop Desmond Tutu defies apartheid laws by walking alone on a South African beach.

August 20, 1619, the first group of twenty Africans are brought to Jamestown, VA. (Read the 1619 Project by Nikole Hannah-Jones).

August 21, 1904, William "Count" Basie, jazz pianist and musician, is born.

August 22, 1917, John Lee Hooker, blues singer and guitarist, is born.

August 25, 1925, Brotherhood of Sleeping Car Porters is founded.

August 25, 1927, Althea Gibson, the first African American Wimbledon tennis champion, is born.

August 26, 1918, Katherine Johnson, physicist, space scientist, and mathematician at NASA, is born.

August 28, 1963, the historic March on Washington, where Dr. King delivered his "I Have a Dream" speech.

August 29, 1920, Charlie "Bird" Parker, jazz musician, is born.

August 29, 1958, Michael Jackson, entertainer, is born.

A rooster is not expected to crow for the whole world.
African Proverb

Doakes and Soaps: The Clean-up Lady
By Rev. Dr. Nathaniel Gadsden

When I first saw the name Doakes and Soaps I was fairly sure that this business sold unique soaps and other toiletries, but I was totally wrong. While interviewing Elizabeth Doakes, the founder and owner of Doakes and Soaps, I quickly learned that most people make the same mistake I made. Ms. Doakes created her unique cleaning business, March 15, 2018, which provides a detailed cleaning service that uses toxic free plant-based products. Doakes and Soaps cleans family homes and businesses with the same attention to detail and professionalism.

Doakes and Soaps currently provides cleaning services in 13 cities in Central Pennsylvania: Dillsburg, Enola, Etters, Harrisburg, Hershey, Highspire, Lancaster, Mechanicsburg, Middletown, Steelton, York and York Haven. When I asked Ms. Doakes how she advertises her cleaning service she quickly said, "By word of mouth, including my commercial businesses." All of her contracted business comes from satisfied clients who rave to their family and friends about how clean their homes are. Clients have called Ms. Doakes a life saver. Her clients love that she will come into their homes and clean them as if it was her own home.

Ms. Doakes has a unique eye for detail. She is especially proud of the plant-based chemicals that she uses to give a top-notch cleaning every time. Ms. Doakes is the sole owner of Doakes and Soaps cleaning service. She is keenly aware that her name is on every contracted service and her reputation means everything to the success of her business.

When I asked Ms. Doakes if she intends to expand Doakes and Soaps in the next three year's she responded by saying "Yes, I plan to eventually move into more commercial cleaning contracts." She went on to say "I created my business because I realized there was a demand to help moms and parents take care of their homes. Cleaning is my gift. There is no better feeling than to come home and being able to relax, and enjoy your home, instead of spending time cleaning up."

Harrisburg PAL: Still Going Strong
By Rev. Dr. Nathaniel Gadsden

The Harrisburg Midtown Arts Center (HMAC) is housed in the former home of the Greater Harrisburg Police Athletic League (HPAL), located at 1110 N. 3rd Street, Harrisburg. As a child I spent many productive, fun-filled hours in the old HPAL building. I remember basketball games, boxing matches, baseball games and weightlifting. HPAL was more than a sports facility, it was a place where young boys and girls learned teamwork, sportsmanship, citizenship, and personal responsibility.   HPAL was a community hub and a very important link between communities of color and the Harrisburg City Police Department. In my youth, Sargent Robbie Lewis was the Executive Director of the Harrisburg Police Athletic League. He was a big man, with a big personality, and a big heart. Sargent Lewis, an African American, was also an active-duty Police Officer, who was well respected throughout the Harrisburg community. His leadership had a major impact on my development as a student, an athletic, and a responsible person in my community.

For a long period of time, the Greater Harrisburg Police Athletic League did not exist in Harrisburg.   The void was greatly felt throughout the community. The good news is that HPAL is back, productive, and once again a major anchor program for youth development in Central Pennsylvania. Dr. Charles Stuart is the current Executive Director of the Greater Harrisburg Police Athletic League. He is cut from the same material as the legendary Robbie Lewis. Dr. Stuart is an educator and visionary with a big personality, and a big heart for helping young people. He is joined by Harrisburg legend, Rev. James "Jimmy" Jones, who provides program guidance, and serves as an advisor to Dr. Stuart.

The Greater Harrisburg PAL program offers programs for youth throughout the year. Programs such as, Mentoring Through Sports (MTS) curriculum, which is modeled after Cal Ripken Sr. Foundation program called Badges for Baseball. The MTS program teaches positive character traits and values that assist youth in becoming positive, productive citizens. Youth participants are encouraged to embrace values, like diversity and responsible behavior, at all-times. Sports activities in baseball, basketball, boxing, and wrestling, are offered year-round to achieve this objective. Special events, such as fishing, bowling, roller skating, and shop with a cop, are also offered throughout the year.

The Greater Harrisburg PAL program also collaborates with The Writer's Wordshop, Inc., a 501 (c)3 non-profit organization that provides a weekly platform for poets, novelist, and writers of all genre, to share their writings. The Wordshop provides writers retreats at Elizabethtown College, Storytelling programs, writing seminars, and publishing opportunities. During the month of December, the Writers Wordshop will offer its Annual Pre-Kwanzaa Celebration at Crossroads Christian Ministries, 350 Harrisburg Street, from 10:00 a.m. to 5:00 p.m., on December 11th. The program is free and will feature cultural performances, speakers, Life Esteem Community Honorees, a fashion show, and vendors of all types. Youth from the HPAL are invited to participate in the Kwanzaa Celebration.

Also on December 11th, HPAL will host its Annual Shop with a Cop program. This is an excellent opportunity for young people, ages 9 years old to 17 years old, to receive some early Christmas gifts, and get to know Police Officers in a whole different light. Parents must sign up for this program at:
www.harrisburgpal.org
Another program available to youth who participate in HPAL is the HAPAL/TRU – Tobacco Resistance Unit. This group of youth take part in legislative conversations regarding increasing the age of young people to purchase tobacco products from 18 to 21 years old. This group promotes tobacco resistance education as vendors at different events, such as the Annual Farm Show in January.

Life-Long learning is at the core of the programs and activities offered by the Greater Harrisburg Police Athletic League. The goal of HPAL is to bridge the gap between the youth mentees and law enforcement officers, with the objective to reduces crime and recidivism in our communities throughout Dauphin County.

HPAL needs your support. You can contribute by giving a financial donation to the organization. Your donation will be tax-deductible. You can become a Mentor to a group of young mentees who are interested in sports, writing and arts programs, community improvement projects, and law enforcement.

If you damage the character of another, you damage your own.
Yoruba Proverb

Let The Word Be Heard!
By Rev. Dr. Nathaniel Gadsden

Then and Now

   We must choose our battles wisely to ensure success both individually and collectively.
24 hours
1,440 minutes
86,400 seconds of my life, trying to control my thoughts. Everyday learning what things are healthy for my mind, body, and spirit, and putting all my focus on them; constantly searching for success, like rock-solid, un-moveable, no doubt about it success!

   One full day! Every minute, every second, every hour of one full day of my life!

I thought about it, but I couldn't define it. My vision, dreams, imaginations were full of past and present steps, missed steps, and relationships that equal ill-tempered, wanton emotional failure.

Success! I can't form a picture of it in my mind. I'm drifting, log-jammed with negative thoughts, wasting my time! One full day – wasted!

   The voice of God, sounding like Maya Angelou, speaks to me, shaking the ground beneath me, with swirling clouds above me, and God says "Africans reinforce positive thought with appropriate behavior, and cast out all negative conditions. Why do you bleed your blessings on useless appendages, like worry and self-doubt?" God says, "Give your time to me. Let go. Gain knowledge of yourself. Learn your truth and follow it. Stay on the path your ancestors blazed for you. Follow the lighted trail of blood, tears, and determination. Commit to the struggle that surrounds you. Let go of the self-made struggle from within. You are already successful. Speak to your ancestors -they are listening and watching always. They will tell you the truth that is yours. Let go of the "I" and grab hold of the "We", as if you are holding Gold. Discover who you really are!"

God, in all of his glory, says "You didn't know it then, when you were wasting your time, but know it now! You can't get back then, so don't waste your time trying. It was THEN that you made hollow, empty excuses. It was THEN that you looked for dead, washed-up scapegoats to devour. It was THEN that you stopped growing, and living like a jagged edge stump, deep in the forest of lifelessness – alone!" Like a broken alarm clock your time stood still. Wake Up!"

God says, "My time for you is moving faster than you can run. You are holding a baton in your hand – don't drop it! You are running a magnificent leg in a vast relay race. You are a force of nature – a part of a gargantuan spiritual body that is guided by my light, so stay the course. Forget about THEN, the wasted time, searching for success. Become one with your NOW! Know that I am with you always. Your ancestors are with me. Stay in your lane. Success is in your DNA. Grip the baton of life. Stay woke, lean forward, be ready to pass it on. Your success is in your hands – NOW!"

(Published in Nathaniel Gadsden's Writers Wordshop Anthology entitled
"Our Words / Our Voices" 2020 on Amazon)

Nathaniel Gadsden's Writers Wordshop, a 501 (c)3 organization, began as an idea to bring a "people's poetry venue" to the Harrisburg area. A chance meeting with Mim Warden, founder of the People's Place Arts organization, lead to the formation of a wonderful relationship with her organization and the birth of Nathaniel Gadsden's Writers Wordshop.
The name, Writers Wordshop (which was supposed to be Writers Workshop), was actually a mistake on Mim Warden's part. While she was completing an application to the National Endowment on the Arts, Mim wrote the word Wordshop instead of workshop, and I decided to keep it. Also, while I was in the process of incorporating the Writers Wordshop, I discovered that there are other organizations named "The Writers Wordshop." On the advice of a good friend, I added my name to

our organizational title, and Nathaniel Gadsden's Writers Wordshop, has been a fixture in the Central Pennsylvania arts scene for the past 44 years.

The Wordshop holds weekly readings, Friday evenings, 7:00 p.m. to 9:00 p.m., on Facebook Live – The Voice 17104 Harrisburg. Poets, spoken word artist, and writers are welcome to join us on Zoom to share their works.   The Wordshop offers publishing opportunities, writers retreats, storytelling programs, free books, Kwanzaa Festivals, Black history programs, original plays, and much more.

The Wordshop is funded by the Pennsylvania Council on the Arts.

We are what our thinking makes us.
Nigerian Proverb

Kwanzaa: An African American Holiday

By Rev. Dr. Nathaniel Gadsden

In 1966, Dr. Maulana Karenga created Kwanzaa and The Seven Principles, he called the Nguzo Saba. The African American Holiday, which is now celebrated around the world, is based on the agricultural celebrations of Africa called "the first fruits" celebrations which are times of harvest, ingathering, reverence, commemoration, recommitment, and celebration of the good.

The Ingathering of the People is a time for the family and of the entire community to renew and reinforce the bonds between them. Dr. Karenga calls this a harvesting of the people, a bringing together of the most valuable fruit or product of the nation, its living human harvest, i.e., the people themselves.

Special Reverence for the Creator and Creation is described by Dr. Karenga as a time of thanksgiving for the good in life, for life itself, for love, for friendship, for parents and children, the elders and youth, man and woman, and for family, community and culture.

Commemoration of the Past Dr. Karenga describes as a time of honoring the moral obligation to remember and praise those on whose shoulders we stand; to raise and praise those who gave their lives that we might live fuller and more meaningful ones.

Recommitment to our Highest Ideal Dr. Karenga calls a time of recommitment to our highest ideals. It is a time of focusing on thought and practice of our highest cultural vision and values, which in essence are ethical values.

Celebration of the Good, Dr. Karenga says is the celebration of the good of life, community, culture, friendship, the bountifulness of the earth, the wonder of the universe, the elders, the young, the human person in general, our history, our struggle for liberation and ever higher levels of human life.

Kwanzaa is officially celebrated from December 26th through January 1st.

Umoja (Unity) To strive and maintain unity in the family, community, nation, and race.

Kujichagulia (Self-Determination) To define ourselves, name ourselves, create for ourselves and speak for ourselves.

Ujima (Collective Work and Responsibility) To build and maintain our community together and make our brother's and sister's problems our problems and to solve them together.

Ujamaa (Cooperative Economics) To build and maintain our own stores, shops, and other businesses and to profit from tighter.

Nia (Purpose) To make our collective vocation the building and developing of our community in order to restore our people to their traditional greatness.
Kuumba (Creativity) To do always as much as we can, in the way we can, in order to leave our community more beautiful and beneficial than we inherited it.

Imani (Faith) To believe with all our heart in our people, our parents, our teachers, our leaders and the righteousness and victory of our struggle.

The friends of our friends are our friends.
Congolese Proverb

Keep Youth Out of Adult Prisons
By: Rev. Dr. Nathaniel Gadsden

The practice of placing youth offenders in adult jails and prisons has long term impact, both on the individual youth offender, and our society. A recent article in the National Juvenile Justice Network Newsletter stated the following:

"Currently an estimated 250,000 youth are tried, sentenced, or incarcerated as adults every year across the United States. During the 1990's – the era when many of our most punitive criminal justice policies were developed – 49 states altered their laws to increase the number of minors being tried as adults. On any given day, 10,000 youth are detained or incarcerated in adult jails and prisons. Studies show that youth held in adult facilities are 36 times more likely to commit suicide and are at the greatest risk of sexual victimization. Youth of color are over-represented in the ranks of juveniles being referred to adult court. In 2008, the U.S. Department of Justice and the Centers for Disease Control and Prevention found that transferring youth to the adult criminal justice system does not protect the community and substantially increases the likelihood that youth will re-offend. NJJN recommends that all youth be processed through Juvenile court."

I fully agree with the final conclusion of the National Juvenile Justice Network. We must keep our youth out of adult courts, jails and prisons. The impact is too great to ignore. I have had first-hand experience with this subject matter on several different fronts. My wife, Patricia Gadsden, founder and Director of Life Esteem Inc., and I, had the honor of working with the Pennsylvania Prison Society in the late 1990's – early 2000's. We taught parenting classes, for five years, at Camp Hill State Prison, Camp Hill, PA. I remember one of the Correctional Officers saying to us that the worst period of time, for him on the job, was the early to mid-1990's. He talked about the young offenders that were placed in this adult facility being some of the most violent, not caring about life, people he had ever encountered. He also said that many of them were greatly abused physically and mentally by the adult offenders on a daily basis.

I enjoyed being the host of a Saturday night radio program on WMSP-FM, at Market Square Presbyterian Church, Harrisburg, PA. For three hours each Saturday night I played soul music, interviewed interesting people, and provided a bit of community news. One of the unexpected benefits of that program was the realization that my program was reaching many of the jails and prisons in Pennsylvania. I start getting calls and letters from inmates and Correctional Officers, requesting that I give a shout-out to family and friends of the inmates. My show became a way for families to connect, especially those separated by great distance. One night a young white man, in his late twenties, early thirties, came to the station to let me know how much he appreciated my show. He had just been released from Camp Hill Prison. He was sentenced there at the age of 14 for murder/man slaughter. He was a 400-pound youth who was picked on by his next-door neighbor, an adult male, who took great pleasure teasing him. One day they got into a physical fight. He told me the man beat him-up pretty badly, until he was able to get the man on the ground and set on his chest. The man could not breathe, and he died. At 14 years old, he was placed in an adult prison where he was picked on, sexually abused, and beat-up more times than he could remember. His purpose for coming to the station was to give me a hand reading the letters and taking calls from the prisons. I quickly realized that at the end of each show he wanted to give a special shout-out to one particular person. He told me that it was this person that saved his life while in prison. He was not much older than himself, but he was tough as nails. It was also clear that my "helper" had become his protector's property, while incarcerated, and there was a mental and spiritual toll that he was dealing with because of the relationship. He also shared with me other such situations, that he had witnessed first-hand, of youth offenders being taken advantage of.

We can stop this unjust practice against our youth. We must keep our youth out of adult courts, jails and prisons for their safety and ours.

Do not call to a dog with a whip in your hand..
Sudanese Proverb

Meet Dr. Ericka S. Pinckney
By Rev. Dr. Nathaniel Gadsden

Let it be known that not everybody who goes to college and receives a professional degree, leaves Harrisburg, Pennsylvania in search of a better community. In fact, there are a-number-of, "home-grown professionals," who have decided to stay in the capitol city of Pennsylvania and give back to the people and community that raised them. It is especially satisfying and very important when African American professionals decide to stay home and give back.

Meet Dr. Ericka S. Pinckney, Clinical Director of Mental Health Services for one of Central Pennsylvania's most prominent human service organizations, Keystone Human Services. Dr. Pinckney is also the sole proprietor of Pinckney Professional Counseling & Consulting Services, LLC, and an Independent Contractor, providing workshops, group facilitation, speaking engagements, resources, community connections, and part-time mental health practice in Harrisburg, Pennsylvania. Dr. Pinckney is a proud graduate of the Harrisburg School District, and Harrisburg Area Community College where she earned an Associate Degree in Secondary Education – Social Science. She also earned a bachelor's degree, in Social Work, with a concentration in Psychology and a Master of Science Degree – Community Mental Health Counseling from Shippensburg University.   Dr. Pinckney is a state Licensed Professional Counselor and certified with the National Board of Certified Counselors. Dr. Pinckney earned her Ph.D. from Walden University in Counseling Education Supervision, May 2020.

I, like many others in this community, have watched Dr. Pinckney grow-up from a beautiful, young Christian lady into a beautiful Christian professional woman. Her smile, friendly demeanor, and caring spirit are the first things that come to mind when I think of this dynamic young woman. Also, I can't help but think of her parents, who have the same kind of spirit and caring nature, when I think of Dr. Pinckney.

Recently, Dr. Pinckney and Rosanne Johnson, M.Ed., LPC, CCTP, NCC, co-founded the Black Therapist of Central PA, a resource to link our community and provide access to culturally specific licensed and pre-licensed clinicians as well as promote clinician networking and support. For more information go to:
https://www.blacktherapistofcentralpa.com/

I am very excited about the creation of the Black Therapist of Central PA organization. For years there has been a major concern in the Black Community that Black people in particular and people of color in general won't go to seek mental health counseling because of the stigma or the lack of therapist that look like them. In an interview with WHP-TV21 News, Dr. Pinckney address these concerns when she stated that many Black people are "suffering in silence," instead of seeking the help they need. She went on to say that "Representation matters to me, and I want to look across the room and see someone who identifies or can experience or maybe feels like I don't have to teach them."

The gift that Dr. Pinckney brings to the Harrisburg community is that she knows the community. Unlike so many professionals who are practicing in the mental health field, Dr. Pinckney is very familiar with the social, political, and economic issues that confront the multi-cultural communities of Harrisburg. She specializes in treating challenging thoughts and behaviors, problem sexual behavior, anxiety, depression, adjustment, grief, loss, and dreams. She is an international traveler, and a mother. Family and friends are extremely important to her, and most importantly, she is a lover and follower of Jesus Christ who she credits as having set the trajectory for her career. Dr. Pinckney is a proud member of Delta Sigma Theta Sorority Inc. and serves as a mentor to young ladies transitioning from High School to College.

Dr. Pinckney is a very successful Therapist. In fact, she currently is not accepting new clients in her private practice because her roster is full. She is able to make referrals and provide resource information to persons and families in need.

Miriam Makeba
"Mama Africa"
By Rev. Dr. Nathaniel Gadsden

On July 16, 1963, South African singer, in exile, Miriam Makeba gave a sobering speech to the United Nations on behalf of the South African people. She said, "My country has been turned by the government into a huge prison." Makeba was speaking about the mass incarceration of thousands of her fellow African freedom fighters, who were determined to dismantle the racist system of apartheid in South Africa. African National Congress leaders Nelson Mandela and Walter Sisulu were two of the most noted persons to be in prisoned and banned by the White racist government. Miriam Makeba was fully aware that her speech would not be well received in her homeland. Makeba, who was living in New York as an established singer, was refused reentry into South Africa following the 1960 Sharpeville massacre, which left 69 Africans dead and another 180 injured. When Miriam Makeba learned of her mother's death, and the death of two other family members, she tried to return home to South Africa, but was told that her passport had been cancelled. Miriam once said, "I always wanted to leave home. I never knew they were going to stop me from coming back. Maybe, if I knew, I never would have left. It is kind of painful to be away from everything that you've ever known. Nobody will know the pain of exile until you are in exile. No matter where you go, there are times when people show you kindness and love, and there are times when they make you know that you are with them but not of them. That is when it hurts.

During her United Nations speech in 1963, Miriam said, "Most of the world's big powers have only paid lip service to the appeals of my people for help. I must urge the U.N. to impose a complete boycott on South Africa. The first priority must be to stop the shipments of arms. I have not the slightest doubt that these
arms will be used against African women and children."

Zenzile Miriam Makeba, born March 4, 1932, and died November 9, 2008, was a South African singer, songwriter, actress, United Nations Goodwill Ambassador, and civil rights activist who gained international fame. Her vocal talent was first recognized when she was a child, and she began singing professionally in the 1950s, with the Cuban Brothers, the Manhattan Brothers, and an all-woman group called the Skylarks, performing a mixture of Jazz, traditional African melodies, and Western popular music. In 1959, Makeba had a brief role in the anti-apartheid film, Come Back, Africa, which led to her performing in Venice, London, and New York City. It was in London that she met American singer Harry Belafonte, who became a mentor and colleague.

Miriam Makeba's career and popularity grew in the United States. She released several albums and songs, her most popular being "Pata Pata" (1967). Teaming up with Harry Belafonte she received a Grammy Award for her 1965 album "An Evening with Belafonte/Makeba." In 1968 she married Stokely Carmichael, a leader of the Black Panther Party. Because of her marriage to Stokely Carmichael, she lost a great deal of support among White Americans. The U.S. Government cancelled her visa while she was travelling abroad, leading her and Carmichael to move to Guinea, West Africa. Miriam continued to perform, mostly in African countries. She wrote and performed songs that were more critical of the racist apartheid government in South Africa. After apartheid was dismantled in 1990, Miriam Makeba returned to South Africa. Her international fame was enhanced by her recordings and performances, including an album with Nina Simone and Dizzy Gillespie, and her appearance in the 1992 film "Sarafina."

Miriam Makeba once said, "I look at an ant and see myself: a native South African, endowed by nature with a strength much greater than my size so I might cope with the weight of a racism that crushes my spirit. I look at a bird and I see myself: a native South African, soaring above the injustices of apartheid on wings of pride, the pride of a beautiful people."

Makeba won the Dag Hammarskjold Peace Prize in 1986, and in 2001 was awarded the Otto Hahn Peace Medal in Gold by the United Nations Association of Germany in Berlin, "for outstanding service to peace and international understanding." Mama Africa, a musical about Makeba, was produced in South Africa and premiered to a sold-out crowd in Cape Town on May 26, 2016.

NuBorn Skin: Love the Skin You're In
By Rev. Dr. Nathaniel Gadsden

Gebrum George 11 created a thriving business based on a personal need, and a burning desire to change his narrative. In his own words George states "For as long as I can remember I've had sensitive skin. The soaps I used to wash my face were strategically selected for fear of using the wrong product and ending up with an allergic reaction. If that wasn't bad enough, I passed the sensitive skin trait to my daughters because they, too, have sensitive skin along with eczema problems."

George took matters in his own hands, by researching and exploring ways to alleviate his families sensitive skin problem. Through his research, George discovered what he describes as

"The perfect combination of natural ingredients which yielded excellent results. Not only did my products work, but the benefits were natural and lasting. No chemicals, no synthesized or modified agents – simply all natural ingredients measured, mixed and specially processed."

Since 2016, George has been the CEO of NuBorn Skin, a company that specializes in beautiful skin care and healthy living. You can find his products at the Broad Street Market in Harrisburg, Pennsylvania, in the red brick building. His operating hours in the Broad Street Market are Thursdays 8 a.m. to 5 p.m., Fridays 8 a.m. to 5 p.m., and Saturdays 8 a.m. to 4 p.m.

George is the sole owner of the company and operates with a small-dedicated staff. He formulates and make all the products sold by NuBorn Skin. His business has a loyal customer base that has shared their satisfaction on Facebook.

Andrea Fulton said "The lip balm is the perfect moisturizer by itself or under lipstick. It doesn't dry my lips out. My skin feels so soft after using the 2-part facial cleanser. I really love the natural ingredients."

Charlotte Wertman said "I used the Tears of Hebe cleanser for the first time. Before my skin was rough, bumpy, clogged pores and dry skin. Now it feels smoother and feels clean. The liquid cleanser is velvety and soothing. It was gentle but effective in removing all of my makeup and deep cleaning my pores…"

Sheila Miller said "I purchased TOH and both of the lip balms and couldn't be happier! My daughter and I both have sensitive skin and TOH eliminated the stress of trying to find a facial cleanser that didn't cause a reaction and worked for both of us…"

Arayna Brown said "I bought one of the lip balms, mint chocolate, and I love it. One product I don't have to keep continuously applying. Keeps my lips moisturized. It's Great!!

In 2021 NuBorn Skin established a partnership with Lettie Marie Luxury Aesthetics LLC, in York, Pennsylvania. Lettie Marie sells NuBorn Skin products and offer NuBorn Skin services to her 650 clients. George is determined to expand his business to a broader customer base. Having his products in store chains nation-wide is a goal he is clearly working toward.

You can check-out NuBorn Skin Care Products and services at www.NuBornskincare.com.

Coffee and Love taste best when hot.
Ethiopian Proverb

Nyeusi Print Shop: Black Owned/Black Excellence

By Rev. Dr. Nathaniel Gadsden

There is a brand-new print shop in Harrisburg, Pennsylvania that promises to have great impact in the African American community. Nyeusi (pronounced - Ni Woo See in Swahili) Print Shop is a state-of-the-art print shop, owned by Dr. Dale Dangleben, MD, and operated by Bradley D. Wainwright and his business partner, Isaac Sloan. Dr. Dangleben, a Critical Care Surgeon in Camp Hill, PA., heard of a print shop in Hamburg, PA. that was going out of business. He purchased the print shop and hired Bradley Wainwright and Isaac Sloan, owners of Urban Revolution Marketing, to handle the day-to-day operations of Nyeusi Print Shop.

I had the pleasure of meeting with Bradley Wainwright at Nyeusi, and getting a tour of the facility, which is very impressive, located in an easy to access area, next to the Governor's Mansion on Front Street. Nyeusi offers a one-stop-shop for all your printing needs. The print shop can handle very large printing jobs as well as business cards and flyers. There are screen printers that can produce ten printed shirts at one time. There are heaters that can rapidly put imprints on sweatshirts and hoodies. Brochures, yard signs and election signs and posters are no problem for Nyeusi.

The most unique feature, of the Nyeusi Print Shop, is their ability to provide the services of the Urban Revolution Marketing group. Urban Revolution Marketing and Branding offers Web Design, Social Media Management, SEO, which will help your brand get noticed, Marketing and Branding. Urban Revolution Marketing and Branding, through the Nyeusi Print Shop, promises to work with you to build a web site that will expand your brand. If you already have a site, then they will make the changes that will bring life back to your site. If you don't have a Google business account, they will create one for you. They offer traditional services such as Logo creation, and Business Cards. Also, they will help you target the right customers for your business and manage all of your marketing responsibilities.

Nyeusi Print Shop currently has three full-time employees and two part-time employees. The print shop officially opened, October 11, 2021, and held their open house on October 17th. The owner, Dr. Dale Dangleben, MD, a Critical Care Surgeon at Holy Spirit Hospital, is also owner of Nyeusi Gallery, with partner Michelle Green, 1224 N. 3rd Street in Midtown Harrisburg. Dr. Dangleben is truly dedicated to enhancing the African American community by investing in the culture, health, and development of businesses within the community. Nyeusi means Black or Darker in Swahili. Dr. Dangleben is an author, with 17 published books to his credit. He was born in Dominican, Republic, and came to the United States about 31 years ago.

Bradley Wainwright and Isaac Sloan are both from Harrisburg. Bradley attended the Nativity School and graduated from Bishop McDevitt High School. Isaac Sloan attended Cheyney University where he majored in business management. Bradley's life goal was always to have his own business. Teaming with Isaac to form Urban Revolution Marketing they have provided "visibility, platforms, and partnerships that will attain the much needed and deserved equity that has long been fought for by those who have come before them."

Nyeusi Print Shop promises to be the fulfilment of the dreams and goals of Dr. Dale Dangleben, Bradley Wainwright, and Isaac Sloan. Collaboration and resource sharing has always been one the most effective ways to achieve successful community building projects, that promotes pride, unity, and economic stability, especially in underdeveloped communities of color. What I find so exciting about the creation of Nyeusi Print Shop is that Dr. Dale Dangleben, a highly successful Critical care Surgeon, has invested in the African American community, by teaming with two highly skilled, young African American males, to provide a first-class business, that can greatly assist other businesses, newly formed or well established, regardless of race or cultural identification, to grow and prosper. This model of business collaboration, hopefully, will be duplicated and shared by others who have the skills and resources to make a lasting difference in the community in which they live.

Our Trip To South Africa: Thank You Dr. Yates
By Rev. Dr. Nathaniel Gadsden

It was a part of our bucket-list to travel to South Africa. My wife, Pat, and I have talked about traveling to South Africa for a few years, but we never actually made solid plans to do so. We were introduced to an opportunity to make the trip many years ago, thanks to Mrs. Verna Edmonds and the Rev. Dr. Calvin Edmonds who told us about a wonderful educator from Washington D.C., Dr. Bettye Bouey Yates, whom they had traveled with to South Africa on one of her many group tours that she sponsored twice a year. We always had it in the back of our minds to reach out to Dr. Yates about her South African tours, but the time just never seemed right with our schedules.

This year, Pat came to me and said, the tour to South Africa that the Bettye Yates Foundation sponsors is November 2nd to the 14th of this year, I want us to go. I immediately said let's go. Pat then informed me that Dr. Bettye Yates had died, and this was partly a memorial tribute and tour in honor of Dr. Yates. I was at once sadden to hear that Dr. Yates had died, but excited to know that she had left a legacy through her Foundation and that our South African trip would have added significance. Part of our tour would include a memorial service in honor of Dr. Yates, which would include pouring her ashes in the ocean, outside the city of Durban.

The tour of South Africa was fantastic! The tour was sponsored by the Bettye Bouey Yates Foundation and organized by Harvey World Travel. After a very long trip which included a flight out of Dulles International Airport, Washington D.C., to Doha, in the Middle East, a six-hour layover, and then on to Johannesburg, South Africa, we were ready to realize a long-held dream. We were not disappointed. After enjoying a buffet breakfast at our hotel, and getting some much-needed rest, we boarded a luxury bus and was treated to a tour of Soweto, South Africa's largest city, with 3.5 million people, on the outskirts of Johannesburg. Our tour guide, named Queenie, is a life-long resident of Soweto, and was a part of the Soweto uprising in 1976.

I found her to be a tremendous asset to our full understanding of the horrible impact the system of apartheid had on our African brothers and sisters, and all people of color. We also visited the Orlando Children's Home, an orphanage for abandoned, abused and parentless children. This was one of the institutions that Dr. Yates supported for more than 20 years.

We also visited Pretoria, the administrative capital of South Africa. There we visited the Voortrekker Monument and the Union Buildings where Nelson Mandela was inaugurated as South Africa's first democratically elected president, and where he lay in state immediately after his death in 2013. While in Pretoria, we also visited the historic Freedom Park, which is described as the South African tale in the voice of the South African people. Most importantly, it stands as a beacon to guide all South Africans on the route of hope and patriotism to a proudly united nation.

The Lesedi Cultural Village was our next stop, where we were introduced to the Xhosa people and the Zulu culture. We also had a lesson on the lifestyles of the Ndebele, Pedi, and Basotho tribal families. We were also treated to a very spirited African drum and dance celebration during our visit to the Village.

For me, the most impactful part of the visit was our tour of the Apartheid Museum. In 1948, racial discrimination was institutionalized. Race laws touched every aspect of social life, including prohibition of marriage between non-whites and whites, and the sanctioning of "white-only" jobs. In 1950, the Population Registration Act required that all South Africans be racially classified into one of three categories: white, black (African), or colored (of mixed decent). All blacks were required to carry "pass books" containing fingerprints, photo, and information on access to non-black areas. The Apartheid Museum is a stark reminder of how this law adversely affected millions of people.

I can't explain the entire impact that this wonderful trip provided to us. I can say that when we poured the ashes of Dr. Bettye Bouey Yates, I said out loud, thank you Dr. Yates, and I was speaking from my heart.

Protest and Repercussions
By Rev. Dr. Nathaniel Gadsden

October 16, 1968, Olympic medal ceremony in Mexico City, African American sprinters Tommie Smith and John Carlos step to the podium and are propelled into history. I had just turned 18, and I was addicted to track and field events, especially the Olympics. I was disappointed that John Carlos had taken third place, in the 200 meters, behind Peter Norman of Australia. Tommie Smith won the Gold Medal as expected. The race was between John Carlos and Tommie Smith both were viewed as the odds-on favorites. Peter Norman had not gotten the memo. It was a great race, and the three men were now set to receive their medals and recognition as the best in the world.

I *Remember watching the ceremony with a sense of pride that two African Americans had won medals, showing the world that we are among the best when given the opportunity to participate. I was both pleased and surprised when the American national anthem began to play, Tommie Smith and John Carlos Raised their single black gloved fist, in a Black Power salute, and lowered their heads, looking toward the ground, in protest, to show solidarity with oppressed Black people worldwide. These two African American men had entered-into the political discourse of the 1960s, which was a decade of protest and violence.*

The backlash and repercussions were swift and costly to both men. The 1968 Olympic games were the first time an American television network had broadcast the Games. It is reported that more than 400 million people witnessed the games, and the protest actions of Smith and Carlos. Even though the two men had protested in a very peaceful manner, they were suspended from the U.S. Olympic team and forced out of the Olympic Village. When they returned home to the United States they received death threats, and were called traitors, villains, un-American and unpatriotic. Author Douglas Hartman "Race, Culture, and the Revolt of the Black Athlete: The 1968 Protests and their Aftermath" is a wonderful source of information concerning the impact and cost to these peaceful protesters, Smith and Carlos.

African American athletes and entertainers, who have spoken out against racism and discrimination, have paid dearly for the stance they have taken. The most recent example is NFL Quarterback, Colin Kaepernick, formerly of the San Francisco 49ers. On August 26, 2016, Kaepernick remained seated on the team bench during the playing of the national anthem. This was the third time he had remained seated during a pre-season game. When he addressed the media after the game he reportedly said: "I am not going to stand up to show pride in a flag for a country that oppresses black people and people of color. To me, this is bigger than football, and it would be selfish on my part to look the other way. There are bodies in the street and people getting paid leave and getting away with murder." He went on to say: "If they take football away, my endorsements; I know that I stood up for what is right." Although Colin Kaepernick also announced that he would donate $1 million to charities and stated that "Once again, I'm not anti-American." "I love America. I love people. That's why I'm doing this. I want to help make America better," he was booed by fans, and made a villain by comments from former President Donald Trump. Kaepernick played his last NFL game on January 1, 2017, because he was blackballed by NFL owners.

Basketball Superstar, Lebron James, who has been outspoken on social issues, especially police brutality, was told publicly to "Shut-up and dribble," by T.V. host Laura Ingraham, a Republican and Trump supporter, who once did a segment on her show to explain why Lebron James is dumb. LeBron has not been hurt by the criticism in the least bit. He continues to speak out and give back to his community in many productive ways.

Eartha Kitt, the great actress, best known for her stunning good looks and distinctive voice, took time to criticize the Viet Nam War to Lady Bird Johnson while visiting the White House. She in turn was greatly criticized by the press and her acting career took a major hit. She was blackballed from Hollywood for years.

I say, thank you, to all the brave souls who have used and continue to use their platform to speak up and defend our community against racism and discrimination, no matter the cost.

Examine what is said, not him who speaks.
Egyptian Proverb

Rafiyqa Muhammad: An Agent for Change
By: Rev. Dr. Nathaniel Gadsden

Rafiyqa Muhammad has been a consistent voice for social justice, cultural inclusion, and health equity in the Harrisburg community for more than 35 years. Mrs. Muhammad, along with her late husband Ali, created Ngozi Incorporated, a non-profit, 501(c)3 organization that offered martial arts classes, an independent school for elementary aged students, arts & crafts programs, and a stand in the Broad Street Market, which offered African clothing and artifacts. Ngozi was best known for operating the Annual African Family Festival, which was held the last Sunday of June in historic Reservoir Park, offering an array of vendors, entertainment, educational programs, outstanding community speakers and political leaders. Ngozi Incorporated positioned Mrs. Muhammad to be front and center and a major voice at every segment of the Greater Harrisburg community.

One of the manly talents of Rafiyqa Muhammad is teaching urban agriculture to kids. For years she has dedicated a major part of her life to learning how to garden and grow healthy fruits and vegetables. The passion that drives her desire to garden is the realization that many residents living in urban areas need access to fresh produce. Too many residents, especially children, get most of their nutrition from local corner stores, which offer little fresh produce, but products that contain carbohydrates such as sugars, starches, and celluloses. The consumption of a high carbohydrate diet over a long period of time leads to diabetes, heart failure, high blood pressure and many other long-term illnesses that can shorten the average life span of individuals. Mrs. Muhammad is a certified permaculture instructor. She works with many organizations in the Harrisburg community, offering workshops through her Let's Get Dirty! Urban Agriculture Center.

Currently, she is working with the Camp Curtin YMCA's urban garden program, where she provides hands-on workshops to youth, teaching them how to create raised garden beds, grow vegetables, such as kale, melons and cabbage, and fruits such as strawberry plants.

She has a special interest in getting "Black hands into Black soil." Her goal has always been to teach as many families as possible how to start their own garden at home.

Mrs. Muhammad is more than qualified to fulfill her role as an advocate and instructor of healthy living and nutritional education. She has studied at the Eco Institution, which is an Earth sanctuary and learning community dedicated to healing the human-Earth relationship. She has served as a Consultant at Shady Nook Farms. She is the Former Acting Manager at the Broad Street Market Corporation. She also studied Business Administration at Harrisburg Area Community College. Besides her work as an instructor of healthy living and nutrition, Mrs. Muhammad is a noted African Dancer, entrepreneur, and events coordinator.

Shenita Baltimore, a graduate of Sci-Tech High, Princeton University, and the University of Delaware, said this about Mrs. Muhammad:
"Peace, Queen." That's how Mrs. Rafiyqa greets me.. but that's now that I am a woman. My earliest memories of Mrs. Rafiyqa, however, were when she taught my mom, aunt, sister, and me in an African dance class decades ago. In fact, she performed with my sister and me for a school assembly when I was only in first grade. So, I've known her for a long time, nearly 30 years! I have called Mrs. Rafiyqa more than once with an idea for a community project (usually involving a garden or nature) only to have her tell me, "Oh that's great baby! It sounds like something I'm doing/just did with..." That's her – always on it, always moving and making things happen! So, she's my go-to when I'm trying to care for my garden or seasonally maintenance my yard, sure. But she's also a source of inspiration for achieving balance (in life and nature), committing to service, and having the courage to speak truth to power. In possession of the rare (and often misunderstood) gift of ensuring people know, with her, where they stand, Mrs. Rafiyqa also has a heart of gold and a sincere sweetness that not everyone has the blessing of encountering. I am so grateful to be one of those people afforded her gifts of kindness, realness, and generosity. I love Mrs. Rafiyqa, and our communities are greater, stronger, brighter, and safer because of her love, work, and Warrior Mother Spirit. Peace, Queen."

Reginald F. Lewis, Esq.
"Keep Going, No Matter What."

By Rev. Dr. Nathaniel Gadsden

Located at 830 East Pratt Street, in downtown Baltimore, Maryland, the Reginald Lewis Museum is the largest African American Museum in Maryland.   The museum opened in 2005 and is described as the authentic voice of Maryland African American history and culture. The museum, which is referred to as "The Lewis", is named after Reginald F. Lewis, who was a businessman, attorney, venture capitalist and philanthropist. The Lewis Museum is located two blocks east of the Inner Harbor, and in my estimation, is a main attraction while visiting the great city of Baltimore.

It was in August 1987 that Reginald Lewis structured the $985 million leveraged buyout of Beatrice Foods by his own Wall Street investment firm, the TLC Group.   TLC became the largest African American owned business ever.   Reginald Lewis is widely credited with starting a movement that pushed African and African American entrepreneurs successfully into the global marketplace.

Reginald Lewis was born in Baltimore, Maryland on December 7, 1942. He is a graduate of Virginia State University, 1965, with a degree in Political Science. After participating in a summer program at Harvard University, which was designed to introduce African American students to the field of Law, Harvard University accepted Lewis into their Law School even before he applied to the program. Lewis graduated from Harvard Law school in 1968.

His TLC firm specialized in venture capital development for small and medium-sized businesses. In 1984 he invested $1 million of his own money and acquired McCall's Pattern Company for $25 million. Three years later he sold the McCall's Company for a profit ninety times his original investment. Needless to say, Reginald Lewis was a brilliant businessman who was turning around the notion that African Americans could not compete in a global marketplace. He was quoted in Black Enterprise magazine saying "To carry around the notion that if I fail it's going to mean that no other Black person will ever have a similar opportunity, or if I succeed that it's going to somehow open a floodgate of opportunity for other Black Americans misses the point... I don't want to pay 5 percent more on a deal because we're going to be the first Americans of African descent to do it. If our work is perceived as an indication that Americans of African descent can function in a global competitive situation, that's nice. But I've always believed that anyway!"

Reginald Lewis grew up in a middle-class neighborhood. He worked hard for everything that he earned. He won a football scholarship to Virginia State University. He was accepted into the summer program at Harvard Law school and because he distinguished himself during the program, he was admitted into Harvard Law School. Despite all of his accomplishments, Reginald Lewis never forgot his roots and clearly understood the role he played on a global stage as a person of African descent. I once read that Lewis wanted to make sure that his two daughters, Leslie and Christina would understand their history, the privileges they enjoy because of his success and their responsibility to contribute to society.

Reginald Lewis was said to be a hard working "driven" person who could be difficult to live with at times. His wife, Loida Nicolas-Lewis, is said to have sought the counsel of her mother-in-law on more than one occasion. Loida had worried that Reginald was pushing the family too hard and had considered leaving him during the marriage. Thanks in part to his mother, Loida stayed in the marriage and the family prospered and overcame those dark and difficult times.

In 1993, Forbes listed Reginald Lewis among the 400 richest Americans, with a net worth estimated at $400 million, however, it was in January 1993 that Reginald Lewis died at the age of 50. His death was caused by a brain tumor. His wife, Loida, assumed the position that her brilliant husband built and nurtured through his TLC firm and Beatrice Foods. She carried on his legacy of business excellence, but she also maintained his philanthropic commitments. One of his many "gifts" to his community was his vision to create a museum of African American culture. Today, the Lewis Museum offers educational programs for children and adults, a two-story theater, a gift shop, meeting rooms, an outdoor terrace, and exhibitions such as "Make Good Trouble: Marching for Change", and Freedom Bound: Runaways of the Chesapeake.

Reginald Lewis always said, "Keep going no matter what!"

Those who are absent are always wrong.
Congolese Proverb

She Grabbed Me

She grabbed me like a thug in the night,
  Like a Back-alley sneak attack, Urban gorilla style.

    She shook the shame out of me. I was ashamed that I didn't have my books that were Required for class. I was ashamed that my clothes were wrinkled and stained from two-day old pizza and chicken grease. I was ashamed that some of my classmates had witnessed the source of my shame, my family on full display for all to see – the drinking, the cursing, the fighting, the theater of disfunction and despair – the price of admission – FREE!!

She never said a word as she treated me like a nigga and shook me with all the hate she could manage.

  She didn't ask me if my mother was fighting and fussing all night.
    She never asked me if I knew where my books were. I knew my books were. They were somewhere in the cluttered state of our welfare decorated apartment, with beer cans and wine bottles thrown everywhere. My teacher didn't know, nor did she care to know, of the army of roaches that had taken up residence in our apartment, without a lease agreement or even a fair hand-shake agreement.
    She never asked me if my father even bothered to come home, and if I missed him.

    She never asked me if I was alright after the horrible night at my home without electricity or heat in the dead of winter. She never asked me anything. She never said a word.

    She just shook the shame out of me in front of the whole class, for all to see, and just walked away. We were in the 3rd grade. We were all black except one white kid left behind – trapped.

She was a white-women – called teacher. I was a Black boy, with red-hot hatred Burning inside of me. I lost all shame that day. I was mad and I was determined to shake the Devil out of her one day, but I never did, and I thank God that I didn't.   Prison is the new form of slavery and I choose freedom!

The chameleon changes color to match the earth; the earth doesn't change colors to match the chameleon.

Shirley Chisholm: A Renowned Renegade
By Rev. Dr. Nathaniel Gadsden

Shirley Chisholm, the first African American woman to serve in the United States House of Representatives, on July 13, 1972, at the Democratic National Convention in Miami Beach, Florida, was nominated for the presidency of the United States of America. This was a bold and dangerous move for the Brooklyn-born Barbados Caribbean-American congresswoman. When she first announced her candidacy for the presidency in January 1972, both members of the Black and White political establishments spoke out against her candidacy. No Black person in modern times had made a serious attempt to become President of the United States, and especially not a Black woman.

Shirley Chisholm was fearless and tireless in her pursuit to be a change agent for the betterment of all people, especially people of color. She was elected to the United States House of Representatives from Brooklyn, New York in 1968, the same year that the Rev. Dr. Martin Luther King Jr. and Robert F. Kennedy were assassinated. The country was deeply entrenched in the Vietnam War. As a presidential candidate, her foreign policy platform spoke against the Vietnam War and against white-dominated European and American governments that worked against the complete liberation of African and Asian peoples. Representative Chisholm made it clear that she wanted to put an end to European colonial rule on the continent of Africa. She particularly wanted to overthrow the minority white governments of Rhodesia and South Africa. Shirley Chisholm had announced in 1969 that she was determined to "put American money to use for people and peace, not for profits and war."

Shirley Chisholm was a catalyst for change during her 12 years in Congress. She hired an all-female staff on her first day of Congress, sending a clear message to the "good-old boy system" that things were about to change. She challenged the long-established seniority system in Congress, when she was assigned to a subcommittee of the House Agriculture Committee, an appointment she felt had no relevance to the people she represented in her Brooklyn, New York district. Her protest was upsetting to her congressional colleagues, but she was reappointed to the Veterans Affairs Committee and later, to the Education and Labor Committee. She was determined to live-up to her campaign slogan from 1968, "Fighting Shirley Chisholm – Unbought and Unbossed." This slogan became the title of her first book, an autobiography published in 1970.

We should never forget our history. We should never let others tell our history to us. Our history is full of hero's, educators, builders, warriors, freedom fighters, preachers, and trail blazers. We must remember those who came before us, those who stand with us, and the ones yet to come. Our reference point cannot start with the enslavement of our people, Jim Crow Laws, Black-On-Black Crime, or White Supremacy. WE can no longer celebrate Black History without including our African history, as told by our African Ancestors. Shirley Chisholm cannot be reduced to a footnote once a year during Black History Month, because she represented the spirit of the African who understood that only God is greater than your Self. She was an advocate for civil rights for women and people of color, improved educational opportunities and social services for the poor, and fought against out-of-control defense spending. She fought for abortion rights and would not allow "business as usual" in the House of Representatives or the Democratic Party.

Shirley Chisholm had many accomplishments during her storied career. She was one of the founders of the Congressional Black Caucus in 1969 and the National Women's Political Caucus in 1971. She fought against police brutality and drug abuse. In her second autobiography, "The Good Fight", published in 1973, Chisholm reflected on her campaign to be President of the United States, and said, "I ran for the presidency, despite hopeless odds, to demonstrate the sheer will and refusal to accept the status quo." Because of her tireless and fearless spirit, and reputation as a renowned renegade, the citizens of Brooklyn, New York reelected her to seven terms in Congress. She retired in 1982 from Congress, but not from public service and community activism. Chisholm co-founded the Political Congress of Black Women in 1984 and supported Jesse Jackson's 1984 and 1988 presidential campaigns.

Until her death on January 1, 2005, she continued to speak out on national issues, was a much sought-after lecturer, and taught at Massachusetts Mount Holyoke College and Spellman College. Remember, Shirley Chisholm made "Good Trouble!"   Ashay!

If a mouth turns into a knife, it will cut off your lips.
Rwandan Proverb

Stop The Violence: Is it still a Movement?

By Rev. Dr. Nathaniel Gadsden

September 10, 1987, Nassau Coliseum in the New York Metropolitan area, the "Dope Jam" rap concert tour was the hottest thing in town. Young people, mostly African Americans, from all parts of the tristate metropolitan area were prepared to witness some of the best rap artist in the business. Performers like Kool Moe Dee, Boogie Down Productions, and Doug E. Fresh, rap royalty to be sure, were some of the main headliners. However, the awesome line-up of performers had to take a back seat to the "real show" that unfolded to the dismay of the promoters, fans, and performers. The event was a disaster to say the least.

Two rival gangs, intent on destruction, were among the ticket holders who had plans of their own to put on a show. The rival gangs fought each other, robbed other concert attendees, caused as much destruction to the coliseum as possible, and in the end, left one teen murdered, many persons stabbed, hundreds injured, and a community shaken and afraid.

Rap music was relatively new to the vast and lucrative music industry. From the beginning there was skepticism about this new form of "urban expression" that black and brown youth had embraced. There was even greater concern, from the majority white community, when white youth begin to embrace the music and the styles that represented rap music. The lyrics, which often spoke in very derogatory terms about women, sex, the establishment, and the police, was credited with creating a very angry, hostile, violent generation of young men and women who didn't value life.

After the Nassau Coliseum riot the national press had major headline news stories concerning "rap music violence" and the danger it presented to the nation. The national debate was taking place in all communities, regardless of race, culture, or economic status. Even those communities that had not been "touched" by the rap phenomenon were part of the debate, especially since some of their young people were showing signs of embracing this new form of "anti-establishment" expression.

Strange as it may seem, there was a silver-lining that came out of this terrible event. Rap artist, producers, record companies, and promoters sprang into action, to defend their art. Understanding the tremendous damage that the Coliseum riot did to the reputation of rappers, and the rap industry in general, many of the best-selling rappers of that time signed on to a project that would produce a major historic event in rap music history. Artist such as Boogie Down Productions, Chuck D, D-Nice, KRS-One, and Ms. Melodie brought together the rap community to create an unprecedented collaboration among the Artist. Out of this collaboration new rap music was produced, which lead to a major concert, publishing projects and videos. All of this was accomplished in cooperation with the National Urban League.

There were three major goals for this project to restore the reputation of the rap industry. First, the project wanted to raise public awareness of in-group violence – its causes, cost, and possible solutions. Second, the goal was to raise funds for groups actively involved in preventing crime and ending illiteracy. The Third goal was to present the image of rap as a partner in the positive encouragement of inner-city youth. Together, the National Urban League and the rap industry launched a nation-wide campaign called "Stop the Violence Movement."

The collaboration was a ground-breaking victory for the rap music industry. This project created a series of concerts, a dynamic video and a bestselling book, all focused on the theme: "Stop the Violence – Overcoming Self-Destruction." Writer, Janus Adams said, what this movement really celebrated was an underplayed truth: the initiative and integrity of African American youth. I fully agree with her assessment. Young rival gangs were all the talk of the nation when they rioted at the Coliseum. When young rappers took the initiative to come together, with the music industry and the National Urban League, there should have been a greater appreciation of their effort displayed in the national press.

Needless to say, as successful as the "Stop the Violence – Overcoming Self Destruction" movement was, the rap music industry was still in for some very dark days. The murders of Tupac Shakur and Biggie Smalls, continue to haunt the industry. Even today, many rappers are still associated with drugs, murder, and the degrading of women. So, the question has to be asked – Is the Movement still a Movement?

A snake that you see does not bite.
Mozambican Proverb

THE African Burial Ground

By: Rev. Dr. Nathaniel Gadsden

I remember the protest, the marches, and the news accounts of an historic archaeological discovery, in New York City of all places, concerning African people buried and long forgotten. I must admit that when I first heard of the protest, I didn't fully grasp the enormous unfolding of history that I was witnessing. The African American community in the lower-Manhattan section of New York, when made aware of the discovery, took to the streets to protest the excavation site, which was being prepared for the construction of a thirty-four story office building. On September 11, 1991, the discovery of the African Burial Ground was declared the most significant find since King Tut's tomb. Archaeologist designated the lower-Manhattan site as the long-lost African Burial Ground bearing the skeletal remains of America's earliest Black Community.

Historian, Christopher Moore, writes that the first known person of African descent to arrive on Manhattan was Juan Rodrigues, a free black sailor from Santo Domingo, Dominican Republic, who arrived in 1613, setting up a trading post with the native Lenape people on Manhattan Island. The first enslaved Africans arrived in New Amsterdam (which later became New York) in 1625, as laborers for the Dutch West India Company. Throughout the seventeenth and eighteenth centuries, Africans were an important part of the city's population, reaching a peak of over 20 percent at the middle of the eighteenth century.

Historian Moore goes on to say that on February 25, 1644, eleven enslaved men were freed and given grants of farmland in the dangerous frontier territory north of New Amsterdam. Their wives were granted freedom also, but their children remained the enslaved property of the Dutch West India Company. In time, they were able to buy the freedom of their children.

The farms owned by the blacks spanned the "Negro frontier " or "land of the blacks."

When our Ancestors died they were shut out of the churchyards in the city, so a burial ground for Africans was developed on a plot of land outside of the city. As the enslaved population grew in New York so did the burial ground, eventually covering 6.6 acres or about five city blocks. However, harsh legal restrictions were applied, as no more than twelve persons were permitted in funeral processions or at graveside services and interment was not allowed at night, the customary time for many African burial rituals. Enslaved blacks were required to have a written pass in order to travel more than a mile away from home. For many, that was about the distance from their lower Manhattan homes to the cemetery.

Between 1991 and 1992 archaeological excavation of the African Burial Ground uncovered the remains of 419 men, women and children: almost half of the remains were of children under twelve years of age. In 1999, nine intact human skeletons were found on the southern edge of the historic ground during construction of new sidewalk on Chambers Street. Thousands of citizens each day were walking by or over the burial grounds of African men, women and children whose souls cried out from under neighborhood sidewalks, roads, and buildings.

The Reverend Thomas F. Pike, rector of Saint George's Episcopal Church, said, "the landmark designation cannot undo the fruits of slavery, prejudice, and exploitation that brought the burial ground into existence and later contributed to its convenient disappearance from the city's active memory. Today we are recognizing the lives of thousands of men, women, and children who were African Americans. Their struggles against incredible odds, their capacity to experience joy, hope, and love in a hostile environment have consecrated the soil in which they were buried."

The remains from the African Burial Ground were temporarily relocated to Howard University, in Washington D.C. for analysis.

New York City's Landmarks Preservation Commission designated the site the "African Burial Ground and the Commons Historic District in 1993. Between 1991 and 2003 the remains were given an analysis at Howard University in conjunction with scholars and researchers from around the world.

On October 4, 2003, more than ten thousand participants marched in the "Rites of Ancestral Return" in New York City, to help re-inter the ancestral remains, each in a hand-carved wooden coffin made in Ghana and returned to the site of the African Burial Ground. Nearly 8,000 personal handwritten messages from the living to the African Ancestors were also buried with the remains.

A fully grown-up tree cannot be bent into a walking stick.
Kenyan Proverb

What, So What, Now What
By Rev. Dr. Nathaniel Gadsden

One of my life lessons that has sustained me through many difficult situations, has been acceptance. Once I accept the fact that I have a dilemma, which has impacted my peace of mind, and needs to be addressed, I turn to this simple formula of What, So What, Now What. This basic formula, that poses three important questions, has guided me, informed me, and challenged me to move beyond my dilemma to create a new reality. The truth is, at least for me, when I am stuck in the "heat" of a difficult situation I often over-exaggerate the problem, and I too often narrow my focus to one or two solutions. When my focus is limited, I get anxious and irritable, and I make mistakes in judgement, which ultimately makes the problem worst. I have learned, through trial and error, and wise counsel from elders that, in- order to have peace of mind, you must live in the here and now. You can't wish your problems away. You can ignore the problem, but it will be there waiting for you. You can blame the problem on someone else, but it is still your problem to deal with. You can just do something to get rid of the problem, but that may not be the answer to the problem. My three-question formula works every time, because you keep working the process until you achieve the best possible outcome. It is as simple as that.

Let's unpack the first step, which is the "What?" What happened? What is the problem? What caused this to happen? What do I need to do?

The "What" question is the first step to acceptance. In my fifty years of counseling individuals and families, I am still amazed when I encounter people who can't acknowledge their "very obvious" problem. They seem to say, "What are you talking about?" "What problem?" When non-acceptance is the norm, it is almost impossible to address the dilemma and explore possible solutions. To be clear, sometimes it is hard to accept that you made a mistake, especially when people close to you were warning you that you were going down the wrong path. Pride and ego can be major stumbling blocks to acceptance. In order to move forward you must take that first step and accept that you have a "What?" Don't let shame, guilt, or other people's perception of you deter you.

The second step to unpack is the "So What?" So, what does this mean to me? So, what are the consequences that I am facing? So, what are my options?
The "So What" question is the next logical step in this process. Once you have accepted that you have a dilemma or problem, you need to fully understand the impact this situation is having on your physical, mental, and spiritual well-being. You need to understand if the solution to this situation will impact other people. In the first step of the process the "What" phase, you are engaged in "Telling the Story." You are telling the story to yourself and others whom you care to share the problem with. The Story Telling phase if crucial, because it is in this part of the process that acceptance begins to take shape in you. The problem with the "What" phase is that some people get stuck telling and re-telling the story. Too often, the "What" phase becomes that platform for the "storyteller" to recruit an amen corner for themselves. The "Storyteller" is looking for empathy and sympathy from their amen corner, instead of moving into the "Work phase," which are the next too steps in the process. The "So What" phase is part of the "Work Phase" and the beginning of the inside work. Instead of being outer directed, now one must look from the inside out to fully realize the impact the problem is having, and or, will have on them and others. This is not easy work, because the acceptance of the situation has gotten a little-bit deeper and harder to digest. So now what?

The third and final step to unpack is the "Now What?" Now what do I need to do? Now what can I expect to happen after I do this? Now what resources do I need to accomplish this? Now how will I know that what I am doing is working?

The "Now What" phase is the strategy phase of this three-step process. The "So What" phase is the consideration phase of this process. In the third step full acceptance should be the norm. In this step you recognize that you have a problem or dilemma. You have given consideration, to the consequences of your situation, and now you are strategizing as to what is the best option for you to take at this time. It is almost impossible to get to the third step without working through the first two steps, however there are people every day trying to do just that. That's why we ask the question "What were you thinking!?", When we see people do harm to others or self-destructive things that ruin their lives. If they, or we, would just take time to work through this simple three step-process, the whole world would be a better place for all of us to live.

What, So What, Now What, is just one simple tool that I have learned to use in my own life. It is a lesson that I share with others because I know it works. When you have tried one option and have not gotten the best results, you just start from the beginning and work the steps again. For every problem there is a solution. You may not like the best solution to the dilemma you find yourself needing to confront, but one thing is for sure, it is better for you to do your own work then to have someone decide for you. As a Chaplain, I have worked with many patients in hospital beds and inmates in prison cells who wish they had worked through their three steps at a critical period in their lives. In fact, all of us have experienced a few missteps at one time or another. The good news is we don't have to anymore, and I accept that.

An Engaged Father Matters
By Rev. Dr. Nathaniel Gadsden

This Father's Day, remember to celebrate your father and all the men who have been father-like figures in your life. Think about it, many men are fathers to children whom they have adopted. Men marry women who have children and treat them as their own. Men father children because their parents died. Men who are coaches often become father figures for children. Men who mentor also become fathers to children. No matter how they became fathers we must never forget how important they are to the children they take responsibility to raise. I want to especially highlight the importance of the African American fathers, who historically have been maligned as an absent parent or dead-beat dad. According to the U.S., Census Bureau (2011) one out of three American children live in biological father-absent homes. In other words, the African American father is not the only race of men who don't live with their children in the same home. It is also noteworthy that a study conducted by the National Fatherhood Academy found that although many fathers who don't live in the home with their children, are still financial providers, protectors of their children from harm and danger, teachers who prepare their children to enter-into the world with confidence, and fathers who provides a nurturing environment that gives love and stability to their children. These men are single parents, ex-convicts, former addicts, businessmen, and happily married men with well-paying careers. It is so important to remember the pressure society places on African American men regardless of their educational background, marital status, or economic stability. Consider these facts:
74 percent of Black men say that being married is important, compared with 79 percent of White men.
35 percent of Black adult men are married, compared with 30 percent of white men.
49 percent of Black men have never been married compared with 30 percent of white men.
10 percent of Black men are divorced, the same percentage as White men.
6 percent of Black males are heads of household.
17 percent of Black males live in single households without children.
82 percent of Black men say that having children is important.

89 percent of Black men say that being in a good romantic relationship is important.

97 percent of Black men say that being close to their family is important.

40 percent of Black men report that they have helped a friend or family member with child-care on a regular basis, compared with 17 percent of White men who report the same.

88 percent of Black men believe that racism is a problem in today's society.

Black males are imprisoned are imprisoned at more than nine times the rate of White males.

66 percent of Black men worry about not having enough money to pay their bills.

64 percent of Black men report having loaned or given money to family or friends to help with expenses.

Black men (33 percent) are three times more likely to report having trouble paying their rent or mortgage than White men (11 percent).

African American men are often doing the very best they can to be engaged fathers and husbands, but it's not easy. Far too often society judges the African American father with an unrealistic standard of measurement. To say the least, to be an African American father is complicated. The National Responsible Fatherhood Clearinghouse (2012) gives us some excellent points to remember as we celebrate Father's Day.

Accept the father where he is, not where you think he should be, or where stereotypes may lead you.

Try your best not to be judgmental. Recognize your biases toward men with certain types of issues or circumstances. Remember they are some child's father.

It is the right of every child to be supported by both parents. Let every father you know that they are important, needed, and necessary. Tell them – Happy Father's Day and really mean it!

Porters' House Jamaican Restaurant
"The go to Jamaican spot"
By: Rev. Dr. Nathaniel Gadsden

Located at 1233 N. 3rd Street, in the Broad Street Market unit closes to 3rd Street, Harrisburg, Pennsylvania, Porter's House Jamaican Restaurant is the real deal when it comes to a taste of Jamaica in Central Pennsylvania. The food is prepared with the kind of love and attention that one would expect to receive from an authentic Jamaican cook. The owner and cook, Nadine Graham, delivers the Jamaican flare in her personality, and style of service, that one would expect to receive from a woman born and raised in Westmoreland, Jamaica. She is friendly, colorful, clearly in-charge of her business, and proud of her Jamaican cuisine.

I visited Porters' House twice in preparation of writing this article. On each visit I ordered a few dishes for family. We were never disappointed with our selections, such as rice and beans, curry chicken, greens, cabbage, mac & cheese, and jerk chicken. In a word, the food delicious. I would highly recommend Porters' House Jamaican Restaurant if you are looking for an authentic taste of Jamaica.

Porters' House is located inside of the Broad Street Market, which is often extremely busy, filled with repeat customers who know what they are looking for. The Broad Street Market houses more than 40 vendors, offering all kinds of foods, health care products, bakery items, and much more. The first part of the Market, called the Stone Market, was built in 1863. The second part of the market was built between 1874 and 1878. A large part of my childhood was spent shopping, with my family, in the Broad Street Market. When I think about it, I don't remember seeing African American vendors in the Market until I was an adult. Over the years, the Broad Street Market has added a greater mix of cultural and ethnic variety to its vendor list. A visit to the Broad Street Market is worth the trip.

Porters' House Jamaican Restaurant is open Thursdays, Fridays, and Saturdays 7:00 a.m. to 6:00 p.m. It appears that lunch time is very busy, and you may experience a longer wait during that time.

Keep in mind, the wait is worth it. I personally found that later in the afternoon, there isn't as much "traffic" in the Broad Street Market, and the Porters' House Restaurant is not as busy. I had the opportunity to place my order, have conversation with Nadine Graham, even while she was in non-stop motion, and jot-down a few notes.

The one thing that Ms. Graham told me is that Porters' House is expected to open another location in two months. She is exploring a site on 6th Street, close to McClay, in a building that can house more customers and stay open through-out the week. This is good news for all of her customers who love good Jamaican food. I count myself as one of those customers. I must confess that I am a very picky eater, not known to try new things when it comes to food. I like what I like, and I generally stick to that. Therefore, I may not be the best reviewer for the entire menu, but I was able to read some of the reviews posted. For example, Amy wrote:

"They offer entrée options in three sizes. I like the medium for a food filling meal. The default sides are rice, plantains, and vegetables. I always opt for callaloo and cabbage. Both are excellent. For the meats I've tried the oxtails, curried chicken, curried goat and jerk chicken. They are all equally good. Be sure to opt for the sauce because it's sweet and spicy and flavorful. I've never had anything bad at this location."
David wrote:

"Great jerk chicken and other Jamaican goodies like cabbage and callaloo. Nice family run place, with counter seating and seating in the Broad Street Market. Great prices for quality and portion sizes."
Heather wrote:

"Loved the jerk chicken, curry chicken, and the rice and beans. Big portions and the food tastes really fresh and good. Delicious Jamaican food!"

Every city needs cultural diversity and variety that brings a sense of inclusion and opportunity for growth. Sharing foods from various cultures is always a good way to learn more about the customs, history and traditions of a people. You certainly will learn a great deal about Jamaica when you visit Porters' House Jamaican Restaurant in the Broad Street Market, Harrisburg, PA. Nadine Graham and staff are waiting to serve you!

Claudette Colvin: Before Rosa Parks Sat
By Rev. Dr. Nathaniel Gadsden

March 2, 1955, Claudette Colvin, a 15-year-old, eleventh-grade high school student was arrested in Montgomery, Alabama, for refusing to give up her seat to a middle-aged white woman on a crowded, segregated bus. This incident happened nine months before Rosa Parks, who is widely regarded as the mother of the Civil Rights Movement, was arrested for refusing to give up her seat to a white person on a Montgomery, Alabama bus. Still, today most people are not aware of the heroic stance that Claudette Colvin took, at great risk of bodily harm and even death, to end the "lawful" practice of segregation in the deep south.

Claudette Colvin's arrest was widely publicized throughout the Montgomery community. She was recognized as "There's that girl that got arrested," almost everywhere she went. She was regarded as a hero to many, a foolish girl to some, and a troublemaker to others. From all accounts, Claudette was not a troublemaker, but a serious student and a young person committed to civil rights. She was a member of the National Association for the Advancement of Colored People (NAACP) Youth Council and had formed a close relationship with her mentor, Rosa Parks, secretary of the local chapter of the NAACP.

Looking back on her arrest and conviction in 1955, Claudette said that she would not have done anything differently. She, and her classmates, had been studying the Constitution as a class assignment. During the month of February, they studied the history of brave men and women who had taken a stand against unjust laws. On March 2, 1955, Claudette Colvin had rebellion on her mind. She didn't plan to stage a demonstration on the segregated bus that day, but when the moment presented itself, she decided to take a stand, by staying seated.

Three of Claudette's classmates were sitting with her when the white woman boarded the bus. The woman stood in the aisle because she refused to take a seat next to a colored person. The bus driver looked in his mirror and said, "I need those seats." The other three girls got up and moved back, but Claudette didn't. The bus driver continued to yell at Claudette to give up her seat, but she didn't move or respond to his demands. The bus quickly filled-up with other white passengers, all refusing to set next to the colored girl. After the bus driver couldn't get Claudette to move to the back of the bus, he ask a transit police officer to board the bus and remove her. Once again, Claudette refused to move. The transit police officer informed the bus driver that he did not have the power to arrest her. The bus driver proceeded to the next stop. However, another passenger had boarded the bus totally unaware of the standoff that was happening between Claudette and the bus driver. The new passenger was a neighbor to Claudette named Mrs. Hamilton. She was pregnant and very tired. When the city police officers board the bus and demanded that both women move to the back of the bus, Mrs. Hamilton and Claudette refused to move. Two colored men in the back of the bus got off the bus, allowing two seats to be available. Mrs. Hamilton slowly walked to the back and took one of the seats. Claudette didn't move. When the Officers grabbed her by both arms and began to drag her off the bus, Claudette begin to cry loudly and began to scream "I paid my fare, it's my constitutional right."

Eventually, Claudette Colvin was arrested and found guilty of disorderly conduct, assault and battery against police Officers, and violation of the Montgomery City Code which makes it "unlawful for any passenger to refuse or fail to take a seat among those assigned to the race to which he belongs…" Claudette Colvin was placed on indefinite probation. She appealed to the circuit court, but her conviction was upheld. The local NAACP had supported Claudette Colvin, however, when the discussion concerning a bus boycott to fight her arrest and conviction was on the agenda, it was determined not to proceed forward with the plan, because she was pregnant and unmarried. The local press would have torn her reputation apart was the prevailing feeling.

Claudette Colvin had her arrest and adjudication of delinquency expunged by district court in 2021, with the support of the district attorney for the county in which the charges were brought more than 66 years before.

Come by Here Lord

Come By Here My Lord, Come By Here, Oh Lord Come By Here.
Somebody is crying my Lord, Come By Here, Somebody is Dying my
Lord come by Here., Somebody is lying my Lord come By Here.
Oh Lord Wont you come by here!!

He knocked on my door, softly, as if not to be heard. I thought I knew
him, the brother from the block with the lean to his walk, you know cool
as a summer breeze. Brother-smooth I called him. He looked at me, then
left and then right, and spoke with a whisper raspy voice. "Are you
ready?" His eyes were serious and angry and fixed on me like there was
no light in them. I said, "Ready for what?" He pointed to the Red R on
his white tee-shirt, and he slowly said for Retaliation, retribution, and
revenge. Are you ready? I said, "My Brother what are you talking
about?" He said, "Getting even and making this thing right. It is time
that Black and Brown people stand-up and fight back." We are building
an invisible underground army. So, I am asking, are you Ready for
Retaliation, Retribution and Revenge? We need you, he said in a soft
whisper and then walked away. I watched him as he walked away. He
never looked back. He didn't wait on my answer. He just left. However, I
had a feeling that he was coming back.

I have been thinking. Vengeance is mine said the Lord. An Eye for an eye
makes us all blind said Dr. Martin Luther King.
I have been thinking. How is it that so many unarmed black and brown
brothers and sisters have been shot and killed by Police Officers, and
White Supremist, and most of them are found not guilty. How is it that
two young white men can kill 10 innocent black people in a Charleston,
South Carolina Church and A Buffalo, New York grocery Store and are
taken alive, even though they are armed with many guns and manifestos
of death. Come By Here Oh Lord! I'm still thinking, and I need a word
from you right about now. This stuff got me thinking real crazy Lord,
please come by here. Joe Smooth or The Lord? This thing got me thinking
real hard!

A Memorial on My Bucket List
By Rev. Dr. Nathaniel Gadsden

I have put this on my list of things to do in my lifetime; visit the National Memorial for Peace and Justice in Montgomery, Alabama. The National Memorial is "the nation's first memorial dedicated to the legacy of enslaved Black people, people terrorized by lynching, African Americans humiliated by racial segregation and Jim Crow, and people of color burdened with contemporary presumptions of guilt and police violence." I intend to honor the memory of my ancestors by never forgetting what was done to them, as enslaved people who were humiliated, beaten, terrorized, and murdered. My mission is to work for the creation of the beloved community without whitewashing the truth of our past and present reality. Anyone who questions the need to say, "Black Lives Matter,"
Should do two things, visit the National Memorial for Peace and Justice, located at 417 Caroline Street, Montgomery, Alabama, and read the research produced by the Equal Justice Initiative entitled "Lynching in America: Confronting the Legacy of Racial Terror," which documents thousands of racial terror lynching's 12 states in the Deep South, and many states outside of the South.

In one section of the report entitled "Lynching's Targeting the Entire African American Community," it is reported that most lynching's involved the killing of one or more people, but many lynch mobs often targeted an entire Black community by forcing Black people to watch the lynching's, and then demanding that they leave the community or face a similar fate. The report gives chilling details of Black people who were murdered by a self-appointed mob of white men, usually with no official authority, who took "justice" in their own hands with no fear of consequences. These tactics were also used against African American individuals and organized groups who protested their treatment as second-class citizens.

The report outlines that when Black people moved to communities outside of the Deep South, they were targeted and violently terrorized in response to racialized economic competition, unproven allegations of crime, and violations of the racial order. One example cited is of two Black men named Horace Duncan and Fred Coker, who were accused of rape in Springfield, Missouri. Although both men had alibis confirmed by their white employer, a mob of white men refused to wait for a trial. Instead, the mob burned and shot their corpses while a crowd of 5000 white men, women, and children watched. When I read this, I am reminded that the killing of George Floyd was no anomaly or accident. No, the killing of George Floyd and countless other Black people is the direct result of a historical mentality with deep, deep roots that refuses to go away.

Whenever we think of racial hatred and lynching's we think of the Deep South, however, the report makes it clear that: "The lynching era was fueled by the movement to restore white supremacy and domination, but Northern and federal officials who failed to act, as Black people were terrorized and murdered, enabled this campaign of racial terrorism. For more than six decades, as Southern whites used lynching to enforce a post-slavery system of racial dominance, white officials outside the South watched and did little."

There is also a museum in Montgomery, Alabama, called the "Legacy Museum: From Enslavement to Mass Incarceration," which opened the same day of the National Memorial. This is also on my bucket list to visit. The museum displays and interprets the history of slavery and racism in America, with a focus on mass incarceration and racial inequality in the justice system.

The Memorial is organized in three different sections. The first section is a sculpture by Ghanaian artist Kwame Akoto-Bamfo entitled Nkyinkyim, meaning "twisted," a term referring to a Ghanaian proverb, "Life is a twisted journey." The sculpture, seven shackled figures of all ages and genders interlocked together, is a part of a larger project Akoto-Bamfo began in Accra Ghana.

The second section is called Guided Justice by Dana King. Guided by Justice is a rendering of the Montgomery Bus Boycott during the Civil Rights Movement. King's sculpture reminds viewers that thousands of Black people were responsible for the success of the bus boycott.

The third section is entitled "Raise Up" by Hank Willis Thomas, which gives a powerful depiction of policing in America, and a call to action that the fight for justice and liberation is ongoing.

I hope there is never ending support for this much need Memorial and Museum.

Anthony & Melisa: They Keep Believing
By: Rev. Dr. Nathaniel Gadsden

They make a dynamic couple. They add value and vision to the Greater Harrisburg Area Community. They believe in our youth regardless of all the negatives that are associated with them. They are Rev. Dr. Anthony Burnett and Rev. Melisa Burnett, administrators of the Left Out Organization Program (LOOP), a 501 c 3 nonprofit, established in 2002 by Dr. Burnett. He is the CEO of LOOP and she serves as the President of the organization. LOOP provides services to predominantly minority at-risk youth, who are socially and economically challenged, throughout Greater Harrisburg and many parts of Dauphin County. On a weekly basis LOOP provides services to 200 youth who participate in their After-School programs.

I have had the pleasure of knowing Dr. Anthony Burnett (Duke) and Rev. Melisa Burnett for many years. In fact, I am honored to say that I performed both of their ordination services into Christian ministry. Together they have built an extended family for youth and an outreach ministry that not only saves souls but changes lives as well. Their mission is to serve youth in the community by offering a safe, nurturing, positive environment with structured activities. Their aim is to provide youth with a sense of self-esteem as well as teach them teamwork, that will ultimately lead to personal achievements and a greater sense of personal responsibility. The goal of the values and principles taught in LOOP is to prepare participating youth for a positive future, and to become a productive member of society.

In addition to the LOOP organization, Rev. Dr. Burnett, and his wife Rev. Melisa are Pastors of Kingdom Youth Ministry. Through their ministry they enjoy preaching and teaching God's Word and feeding God's people. Their ministry is open to everyone, but they clearly have a heart for the less fortunate and most needy. I see them well established in the former Allison Hill Community Center, providing their LOOP programs and their Kingdom Youth Ministry. The Allison Hill Center is in an area that reaches the population they serve. It is an area that many people, churches, and organizations have moved out of, but not the Burnett's.

Dr. Burnett is also, Co-Founder of Men United Standing Together (M.U.S.T.), a coalition of men dedicated to inspiring change in the Harrisburg region. The mission of M.U.S.T. is to inspire, educate, motivate, and assist neighborhoods to make positive change within themselves and their community. Pulling men together, especially men who are "returning citizens" after incarceration, is no easy task. Men have a bad reputation as fathers, and members of community organizations. I have witness Dr. Burnett and many other men form a strong bond to let their voices be heard and their work be known. By doing this, they have encouraged other men, who otherwise would not be involved, to get involved with their families and community solutions.

To say the Burnetts are making a difference would be an understatement. LOOP is a 12-month program with two components, after school programs and summer enrichment programs. The after-school program provides activities for boys and girls, ages 6 to 18years of age, Monday through Thursday, 5:30 p.m. to 8:30 p.m. Some of the activities that are offered are homework assistance, tutoring, truancy intervention, mentoring, literacy book club, art programs and Life skills. Students come from over 40 different buildings in the region.

The summer enrichment program offers evening camps at Emerald Street playground, and Reservoir Park in Harrisburg. Also, the summer enrichment camps provide a variety of activities such as recreational activities, exercises, drug and alcohol prevention programs, and field trips. The summer programs are offered Monday through Friday 5:30 p.m. to 9:30 p.m.

The Burnetts have a motto, Keep Believing, which they live by every day. Too many people have given-up on our youth, especially those who are most at-risk, but not the Burnetts. They work together and gather support from big-hearted parents and members of the community who believe in the work they are doing, which is to provide a safe and nurturing environment for our youth to play and learn. The Burnetts take Christ and their love for one another with them wherever they go. This is the formula that keeps them believing in our youth. God bless them!

How I Enter Matters
Chaplain Nathaniel Gadsden

I discovered a very important lesson in life a long time ago, how you enter-into a space, a conversation, a relationship, a business deal, or a tragic situation, it truly matters what the outcome will be. As a Chaplain this simple fact has served me well. How I enter-into a relationship with a patient, co-worker, staff member, or family member is up to me. My attitude, sense of well-being, sense of security, ability to be present in the moment, and spiritual motivation will all play a significant part in the relationship between the person I encounter, no matter how long or short the encounter is.

To paraphrase Chaplain Norberto Guzman, Signet Bible College and Theological Seminary, "The Chaplain, as a representative or ambassador of God, is privileged to stay with someone emotional, physical, or in spiritual pain, without trying to fix the person's problems, offer unsolicited advice, or recite religious platitudes. Being present in a time of crisis offers tremendous moral support, the fact that the Chaplain is there may enable them to believe that God has not abandoned them and communicates God's assurance, "Fear not, I am with you." (Isaiah 41:10, NKJV).

I wear the badge announcing that I am a Chaplain. If I am in the dining area, on the elevator, in my office, or doing rounds, there is a clear expectation that I am a representative of God by most of the people I will meet. They don't have to speak to me, or acknowledge me in any manner, but when we enter-into a casual or extended relationship it matters how I present myself to be an ever-present help for God. I remind myself of this every day because it really matters to me.

Pandemic Diary

The door to the Chapel has a distinctive Sound.
It moves slowly as it opens and slower as it closes.
It breaks the silence of the Prayer and the meditator and the griever.
It pushes and pulls out to the hospital hallway always presenting a danger to anyone passing by too close, especially if their hands are full or their minds are elsewhere.

My small office is inside the Chapel. I hear the prayers, the anguished cries, the silence of despair. I occasionally hear the nervous laughter of waiting family and friends who are not allowed to visit their loved ones because, like everything else, the rules of engagement have changed.

On this day the Chapel door opens, but the sound is different. The high-pitched cry drowns out the distinctive sound of the door. The cry is loud and gut wrenching. The cry is telling a story. I don't know the beginning or the ending of this story, but I have heard this story before.

I sat for a minute listening, leaning forward in my chair, frozen and lasered into the sound of the cry.

I opened my office door, walked toward the sound, the cry, the storyteller in despair. I introduced myself as the Chaplain. I spoke with an empathetic voice with the hope that he would allow me to enter-into his story.
"She would not take the shot and now she has the virus." He said, trying to catch his breath. "My daughter also has the virus, because she followed everything my wife told her about the shots." He talked and I listened. He was a master - storyteller and I felt his pain, his anger, and his despair.

" I don't want them to die," Is what I hear him say most. Together, we prayed and prayed, and prayed to the Father, The Son and the Holy Ghost. He told me how much he loved his wife, and he spoke with conviction. His face lit-up and sparkled through the tears of sadness, which were ever flowing. He was present with me physically, but his spirit was in the room with his wife, the absolute love of his life.

He looked at me, and said after a long pause, my wife and daughter cannot die. They are all I have, to live for. I didn't have to say a word. I couldn't find the words to say.

He stood up like a weight was pulling his shoulders down. He was bent inside and out. We hugged and shook hands. I gave him my blessed assurance that I would be there for him and his family, as an ever-present help for the Lord. The distinctive sound of the door sent him on his way.

The next day his wife died, and we cried together. He said, "the last thing she said to me was, I am sorry." By the grace of God, 14 days later his daughter was released from the hospital. I was honored to see him smile. He said thank you brother. And my black hand and his white hand clasp together, strong, and I said, "No, thank you brother, and may God be with you." And I was sure, God was!

You Don't See What I See
By Nathaniel Gadsden

I see the Dry Eyes of Myrlie Evers enduring the unspeakable with dignity, "so those who wished him dead (Medgar Evers Her courageous husband) would not see weakness in her eyes."

I see the photos of Ernie Sisto recording the 1971 protest of NEGRO the National Economic Growth and Reconstruction Organization, outside of the New York Times building. There, in the midst, of this rainbow coalition of united, unwavering, voices of protest stood Thomas W. Matthew, a neurosurgeon, atop a car, proclaiming to all who could hear him the New York Times was more interested in reporting on black violence than on black productivity.

I see Rev. A. Kendall Smith, in 1967, gleefully burning the symbol of enduring racism, the confederate flag, in City Hall Park in Manhattan. Rev. Smith was "protesting the Southern treatment of black residents in New York City." He was later arrested even though no law was broken. This is the history you don't see. The untold history of people who look like me.

I see the heart of Tyrone Dukes, the Times photographer, who had an eye for black excellence. There, walking the sidewalks of Harlem, white skirts and blouses, white head coverings, sisters from the Nation of Islam, escorting young sisters in training to the Muslim school and mosque. Respect, intelligence, dignity, and purpose on full display. Dukes saw what you can't see, because you want to squint at history, when it comes to people that look like me.

I see Bessie Wright of Benedict College and Mary Leach of New York City, workers in a pilot program called Domestic Peace Corps. In 1963, they were among 27 volunteers dispatched to Harlem that summer to work, in a number of different roles such as hospitals, schools, churches, and senior centers. This program led to the creation of a national service program called Volunteers in Service to America or VISTA.

American History, World History, Black History, call it what you want, because it's just history I see, the history of a people that look like me. Oh Yes, People that you don't seem to see, unless you are talking about poverty or slavery.

And the greater tragedy just may be, there are too many people who look like me, who only can see what you can see, who will always be, what you don't see, and they don't even know it's a tragedy. My God! They don't know, not knowing their own history is a tragedy. In order to teach them we have to reach them. And I realize if it is to be it's up to me. Do you see what I am saying? Will you help me? Harambee! Let's teach together our history for all to see!

www.ingramcontent.com/pod-product-compliance
Lightning Source LLC
Chambersburg PA
CBHW081148170626
46809CB00010B/3133